ΔD Architectural Design

Green Architecture

Guest-edited by Brian Edwards

⊛WILEY-ACADEMY

Architectural Design
Vol 71 No 4 July 2001

ISBN 0-471-49193-4
Profile No 152

Editorial Offices
International House
Ealing Broadway Centre
London W5 5DB
T: +44 (0)20 8326 3800
F: +44 (0)20 8326 3801
E: info@wiley.co.uk

Editor
Helen Castle

Exexcutive Editor
Maggie Toy

Production
Famida Rasheed

Art Director
Christian Küsters ↳ CHK Design

Designer
Owen Peyton Jones ↳ CHK Design

Freelance Assistant Editor
Corinne Masciocchi

Advertisement Sales
01243 843272

Photo Credits
AD Architectural Design

Abbreviated positions
b=bottom, c=centre, l=left, r=right, t=top

Cover image: Digital Imagery © copyright 2001 PhotoDisc, Inc.

p 4 courtesy Lindsay Johnston, photo: Peter McNeill; p 6 courtesy Future Systems, photo: © Richard Davies; p 8 © Michael Hopkins and Partners, photo: Richard Davies; p 9 photo: © Brian Edwards; p 10 RIBA Library Photographs Collection; p 11 courtesy Future Systems, photo: © Richard Davies; p 12 © Studio E Architects Ltd, photo: Dennis Gilbert; p 13 photo: © Brian Edwards; p 14 © Michael Hopkins and Partners, photo: Martine Hamilton-Davies; p 15 © TR Hamzah & Yeang Sdn Bhd; p 16 photo: © Brian Edwards; p 18 © Burg & Schuh, Palladium Photodeign, Cologne/Germany; p 19 photo: © Richard Davies; p 20 photo: © Brian Edwards; p 22(t) © Edward Cullinan Architects; 22(b) courtesy of Penoyre & Prasad, photo: © Dennis Gilbert; p 24(tl) & (tr) Foster and Parters, images: Nigel Young/Foster and Partners/Foster and Partners Visualisation; p 25(l) © British Steel; p 25(r) © Richard Bryant/Arcaid; p 26(l) © Buro Happold/Adam Wilson; p 26(r) photo: © Brian Edwards; p 28–9© Renzo Piano Building Workshop; p 33(tl) © Foster and Partners, photo: Richard Davies; p 33(tr) © Foster and Partners; p 33(cr) © Foster and Partners, photo: Nigel Young; p 33(b) © Foster and Partners, photo: Nigel Young; p 34(t) courtesy Future Systems; p34(b) courtesy Future Systems, © Richard Davies; all p 35 courtesy Future Systems, © Richard Davies; p 36(t) © Richard Rogers Partnership, photo: Dan Stevens; p 36(b) © Richard Rogers Partnership, photo: Christian Richters; p 37(tl) & (tr) © Richard Rogers Partnership, photo: Katsuhisa Kida; p 37(cr) © Richard Rogers Partnership; p 37(b) © Richard Rogers Partnership, image Hayes Davidson; p 38 ECD Architects, photo: Peter Cook; p 39 © Peter Cook/View; p 40 © Herzog + Partner, photo: R Schneider, Herzog-Loibl; p 41 courtesy Chetwood Associates, photo: © Cloud Nine Photography; pp 42–3 © Edward Cullinan Architects, images: Hayes Davidson; p 44 © Buro Happold/Adam Wilson; pp 46–7 & 49 © MAS Architects; p 50 photo: © Chrisna Plessis; p 51 © Etienne Bruwer/Greenhaus Architects; p 52 © Bligh Voller Nield, photo: Patrick Bingham-Hall; pp 54–5 © Peter Sutchbury, photo: Tim Linkins; p 56(t) © Bligh Voller Nield, photo: Patrick Bingham-Hall; p 58 © Charles Start University, photos: Derek Swalwell; pp 60–1 © TR Hamzah & Yeang Sdn Bhd; pp 63–7

© Clive Briffet; pp 68-9 © Antony Ng Architects Ltd; p 70 © Rocco Design Ltd; p 71 © Simon Kwan Associates Ltd; p 73 © Leigh + Orange Ltd; p 74(t) © Herzog + Partner, photo: Stefan Moses; p 74(b) © Herzog + Partner, photo: Demuss; p 75 (tl) © Herzog + Partner, photo: Seewald; p 75(tr) © Herzog + Partner, photo: Herzog-Loibl; p75(b) © Herzog + Partner, photo: R Schneider; p 76 © Beeld en Grafisch Centrum TU Delft; pp 78 & 79(l) © Gemeente Rotterdam, photos: Peter Van Roon, Rotterdam; pp 79(r) & 80(l) © CV de Componist; p 80(r) and p 81 © Beeld en Grafisch Centrum TU Delft; pp 82, 83 & 85 © William T Bruder Architect, photo: Bill Zimmerman; p 86 © Scott Frances/Esto; pp 88–9 & 90 © Patkau Architects Inc, photos: James Dow; p 91 © Busby & Associates Architects, Ltd, photos: Martin Tessler.

AD Architectural Design +
pp 94–5+ all photos © Thomas Deckker, except the photos of Congresso Nacional and the Labour camp, which are Arquivo Publico do Distrito Federal; p 96+ © Herbie Knott/Rex Features; p 98+ (tl) © Peter Cook/View; rest of p 98+ © Anthony Hunt Associates Ltd; p 99+ courtesy Nicholas Grimshaw & Partners, © FOILTEC; p 100+ © Nicholas Grimshaw & Partners; p 101+ courtesy Zombory-Moldovan Moore, photo of house: David Grandorge; p 102+ © Zombory-Moldovan Moore, photo: Edward Woodman; p 103+ © Zombory-Moldovan Moore, photo: David Grandorge; p 104+ © Zombory-Moldovan Moore, photo: Andreas Schmidt; pp 105+ courtesy Zombory-Moldovan Moore; pp 106–7+ © Zombory-Moldovan Moore, photo: David Grandorge; p 111+ photo: © Edwin Heathcote

6
24
36
46
52
68
82

Cover image: Digital Imagery © copyright 2001 PhotoDisc, Inc.

Subscription Offices UK
John Wiley & Sons Ltd.
Journals Administration Department
1 Oldlands Way, Bognor Regis
West Sussex, PO22 9SA
T: +44 (0)1243 843272
F: +44 (0)1243 843232
E: cs-journals@wiley.co.uk

Subscription Offices USA and Canada
John Wiley & Sons Ltd.
Journals Administration Department
605 Third Avenue
New York, NY 10158
T: +1 212 850 6645
F: +1 212 850 6021
E: subinfo@wiley.com

Annual Subscription Rates 2001
Institutional Rate: UK £150
Personal Rate: UK £97
Student Rate: UK £70
Institutional Rate: US $225
Personal Rate: US $145
Student Rate: US $105

AD is published bi-monthly. Prices are for six issues and include postage and handling charges. Periodicals postage paid at Jamaica, NY 11431. Air freight and mailing in the USA by Publications Expediting Services Inc, 200 Meacham Avenue, Eimont, NY 11003

Single Issues UK: £19.99
Single Issues outside UK: US $32.50
Order two or more titles and postage is free. For orders of one title ad £2.00/US $5.00. To receive order by air please add £5.50/US $10.00

Postmaster
Send address changes to AD c/o Expediting Services Inc, 200 Meacham Avenue, Long Island, NY 11003

Printed in Italy. All prices are subject to change without notice.
[ISSN: 0003-8504]

94+
96+
101+
109+
111+

4   Editorial   *Helen Castle*

6   Introduction   *Brian Edwards*

8   Snakes in Utopia: A Brief History of Sustainability   *Brian Edwards with Chrisna du Plessis*

20   Design Challenge of Sustainability *Brian Edwards*

32   Lord Foster of Thames Bank – Green Questionnaire

34   Jan Kaplicky of Future Systems – Green Questionnaire

36   Lord Rogers of Riverside – Green Questionnaire

38   Global Perspectives: Learning from the Other Side   *Chrisna du Plessis*

46   Bringing Together Head, Heart and Soul –

Sustainable Architecture in South Africa   *Chrisna du Plessis*

52   The View from Australia: Green Limits in a Land of Plenty   *Lindsay Johnston*

60   Ken Yeang – Green Questionnaire

62   Sustaining Interactions Between the Natural and Built Environment in Singapore   *Clive Briffet*

68   Green Architecture in Hong Kong, the Densest City in the World   *Edward Ng*

74   Thomas Herzog of Herzog and Partner – Green Questionnaire

76   Sustainable Design in The Netherlands   *Ellen van Bueren and Chiel Boonstra*

82   Green Architecture in North America   *Brian Carter*

Green Architecture
Guest-edited by Brian Edwards

𝄐   Architectural Design +

94+   In the Realm of the Senses   *Thomas Deckker*

96+   Building Profile: The Eden Project   *Jeremy Melvin*

101+   Practice Profile: Zombory-Maldovan Moore   *Helen Castle*

109+   Book Reviews

110+   Highlights from Wiley-Academy

111+   Site Lines   *Edwin Heathcote*

As sustainability enters the mainstream, becoming the accepted goal if not always practice of governments and architects alike, it seems to be slipping through our fingers. No longer an alternative route out in the cold, green architecture is, as a result, ever more elusive and difficult to define. With increasing numbers claiming it for themselves, it is no longer possible to describe it in counterpoint – purely in terms of what it clearly is not. It seems to be everything for everyone who wants it – the Queen and President of the RIBA included.

In this important issue of *Architectural Design*, the guest-editor, Brian Edwards, has created an essential survey that in the widest and most specific sense looks at what it means to be green. By bringing together contributors from six differing geographical regions – South Africa, Australia, Singapore, Hong Kong, The Netherlands and North America – a view is yielded that is simultaneously global and local. In South Africa, for instance, Chrisna du Plessis shows sustainability to be rooted in an existing ecosystemic world view that is part of its pastoral and agriculturist heritage, whereas, in contrast, in North America, Brian Carter describes how the design of 'green' buildings is limited rather than aided by cultural factors, particularly society's adherence to the power of industry and commerce. This comprehensive world view is shored up by three introductory chapters by Brian Edwards and Chrisna du Plessis, which sum up green architecture's history and its design challenges, as well as the varying global perspectives involved. By interspersing the issue with interviews or 'Green Questionnaires' from world-leading architects – Lord Foster, Thomas Herzog, Jan Kaplicky, Lord Rogers and Ken Yeang – green architecture is also presented at the point at which it is an individual expression.

What is clear is that there is no still point of the turning world, as far as green is concerned. Variations are thrown up by social, political, cultural and economic factors, as well as by individual preferences. What this issue does provide, however, is some indication of the full spectrum of perspectives that exist under this over-arching umbrella term. ◭ *Helen Castle*

Opposite
Lindsay Johnston, Four Horizons Eco Lodges, Watagan National Park, Hunter Valley, Australia, 2000. This is one of three detached holiday lodges, which are dotted along a cliff top in eucalyptus forest. Orientated towards the morning sun in winter they each have a fabric canopy and roof overhangs which provide shade from the midday summer sun. 'Green' features include a corrugated steel double 'parasol' roof with a 300-millimetre air gap to neutralise solar heat gain, internal thermal mass in concrete floors and blockwork walls which are insulated externally and clad in corrugated iron to keep the buildings cool in summer and warm in winter. Electricity is supplied from photovoltaic solar panels and rainwater is collected in tanks on the roof.

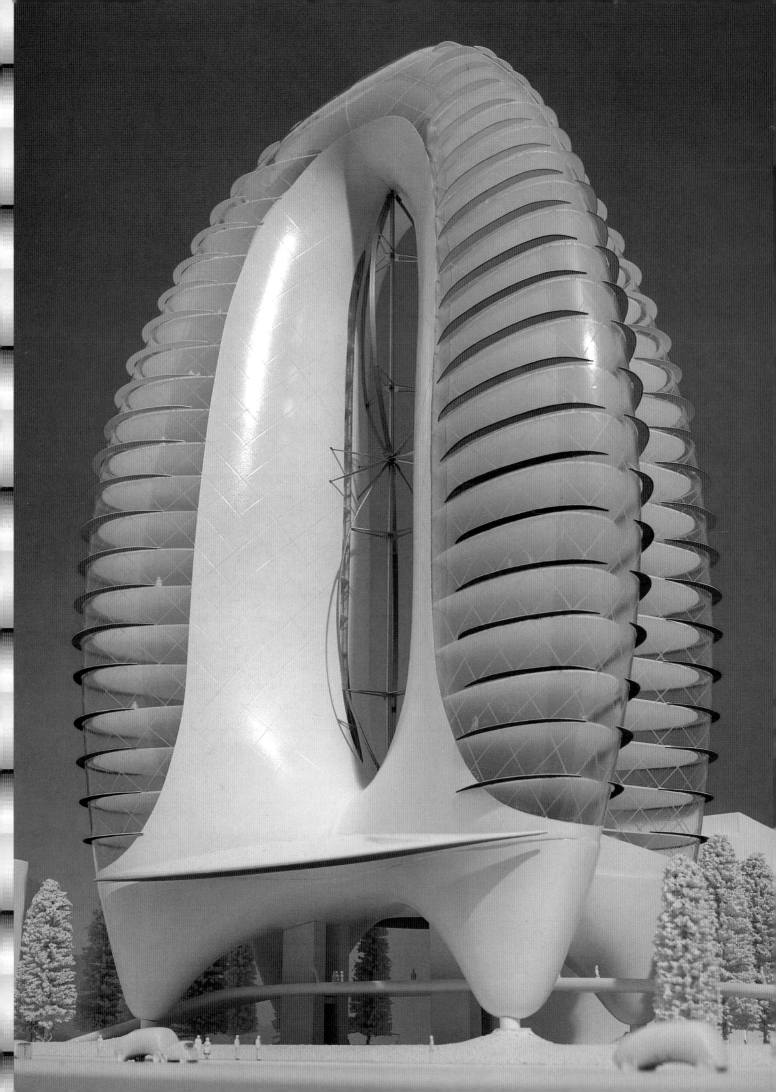

Sustainability: the Search for an Earthly Paradise

This issue of Δ has been developed in order to substantiate the argument that the agenda of sustainability is leading, not to a single universal style but to a rich and complex architectural order around the world. Most books or journals illustrate green projects without highlighting cultural, social and environmental differences. In so doing, this issue has set out to further demonstrate:

• The existence of regional differences in both the philosophy of sustainability and its practice.

• The way sustainability addresses not only global problems (such as climate change) but also local environmental issues (such as township regeneration).

• The existence of high-tech and low-tech solutions, often used in partnership in a single project.

• The way space (the medium of architecture) is altered by sustainability.

The main argument made by the international array of contributors to this issue is that a diverse interpretation of sustainable design exists around the world. The forces which lead to this complexity – climatic, cultural, professional and social factors – can too easily be overwhelmed by the internationalism of sustainability as evidenced by scientific literature. A more appropriate greening of practice occurs when both local and global issues are balanced.

In this issue, examples of multicultural, multidisciplinary building design are drawn from six diverse regions of the world: South Africa, Australia, Singapore, Hong Kong, The Netherlands and North America. The wide geographical spread allows relatively unknown work to be brought to public attention. It also provides the chance to let work from distant lands (South Africa, Australia) inform practice elsewhere, giving a fresh perspective on ecological architecture from countries normally outside critical gaze.

There is an important distinction to be made between low-energy and ecological design. In countries where energy is less of an issue than rainforest protection or water conservation, the concept of sustainability provides a framework for integrated decision-making. Out of this comes a new architectural order and vocabulary which addresses urban layout, the building plan and section, material use and building servicing. Each is altered by the local agenda of sustainability and each will be explored by experts who know the practice in their country.

The new 'sustainability order' is not universal but, like classicism, is modified by regional circumstances. It is an order of process and thought necessarily adjusted by local circumstances – the rightness of sustainability and its cultural relevance relies upon the celebration of difference. In this sense my task as editor has been to search out the particular, showing how cultural traditions, political agendas, craft skills and local technologies are connecting with sustainability to form a rich and diverse global architecture for the 21st century. Δ *Brian Edwards*

Opposite
Future Systems, Project Zed, London, 1995. This innovative and imaginative design for a mixed-use building applies both high-tech and low-tech solutions inventively. Predominantly naturally ventilated as well as naturally lit, Project Zed's form and design are contrived so as to maximise the wind and the sun as free energy sources. Over the course of a year, the building would be almost entirely self-sufficient in energy terms. Formed around a central opening which acts as a wind concentrator, its wind turbines are designed to generate a significant percentage of free energy. The turbines are supplemented by photovoltaics which are integrated into the external shading fins.

Snakes in Utopia
a Brief History of Sustainability

Brian Edwards, with Chrisna du Plessis, gives a brief overview of the green movement, tracing the preoccupation with nature in architecture back to the 19th century. More far-reachingly Edwards and du Plessis explain why, to be effective, sustainability has to be politically subversive. For it not only calls into question the accepted world 'order' – the predominance of 'developed' economies over 'undeveloped' ones – but also the received economic world-view and over two centuries of industrial philosophy.

The roots of the environment movement can be traced back to the 19th century. John Ruskin, William Morris and Richard Lethaby all in their different ways questioned the assumption that industrialisation would satisfy mankind's physical and spiritual needs. Ruskin in *The Seven Lamps of Architecture* called for development to be modelled upon the harmonic order found in nature. Morris advocated a return to the countryside with implications for self-sufficiency and a revival of local craft skills. Lethaby, in one of several rhetorical statements, called on architects to recognise the beautiful order of nature. All three used the term 'nature' but today one can usefully substitute the word sustainability. The 19th century closed with the emergence of a clear, sustainable design movement.

Patrick Geddes in Scotland, Buckminster Fuller and Frank Lloyd Wright in the USA, Hassan Fathy in Egypt and, more recently, Richard Rogers and Norman Foster in the UK have all developed the ideas of these pioneers. But their responses have been quite different. Nature has been replaced by low-energy design because of the immediate and pressing problem of global warming. Whereas Rogers and Foster have developed fresh prototypes for energy-efficient offices, schools and even airport terminals, an opposing thrust of 20th-century designs has been towards improving the environmental condition of urban areas generally. This has found expression in climate-modified cities where an umbrella of glass or plastic has kept heat in and cold out. Geddes and Fuller argued that within such urban areas crops could be grown and a benign nature brought into direct contact with the human race. Fathy and Wright took a different approach: both sought to

Archigram's walking city and organic urbanism were extreme green visions predicated upon the notion of migrating species and the integration of complex ecological and architectural orders.

use local materials and crafts in an endeavour to produce a modern architecture out of regional building traditions. In the process they introduced us to the idea that social sustainability and ecological design were closely related. Archigram, too, in the early 1960s sought a distinctive reconciliation between high technology and environmental problems. Herron's walking city and Chalk's organic urbanism were extreme green visions predicated upon the notion of migrating species and the integration of complex ecological and architectural orders.

The flame of the green movement never really expired in spite of the material excesses of the modern movement. High Tech, the major flowering of modernity in Britain, had managed by the 1990s to embrace sustainability. The close of the century witnessed a fascinating blend of building design, known as eco-tech or eco-cool, that embraced precision engineering, computing and ecology. Buildings ceased to be fixed heavyweight objects but became lightweight, stretched, flexible and in part mobile. As Rogers noted, buildings should be like birds which ruffle their feathers and change their shape and metabolism to suit different environmental conditions.[1] This responsive form of design bridged the worlds of man and nature successfully and gave final built expression to the predictions of Ruskin, Morris and Lethaby. In this, Future Systems have been surprising champions.

Adopting a bigger frame of history, it is possible to argue that pockets of good sustainable practice existed throughout the medieval period in the West and still survive in relatively undeveloped areas of the East and South. The monasteries of Europe produced their own food, created buildings from local materials, captured and recycled water, and developed renewable energy technologies (in the form of water mills and windmills). These were structured societies which took care of the sick and old, cultivated the land according to ecological principles and farmed fish, birds and animals with humanity. Such practices can still be found in rural communities in Latin America, Africa and Asia. Sustainable development is not a term one hears in such settlements, but in reality these are places from which the rest of humanity could usefully draw lessons rather than seeking to 'improve' them.

The Enlightenment in Europe promulgated a scientific rationalist view of the world. It has survived to the present in the mechanistic perception of sustainability shared by most architects and engineers in the West. This finds expression in the focus upon energy, fossil fuels, indicators and definitions. The West tends to 'measure' sustainability whilst the South and East simply 'feel' it. Asia and Africa act out good green practices by instinct, and their point of reference is not Newton or Einstein but the local shaman or wisdom keeper. It is one of the ironies of the modern world that the societies which talk most about sustainability (the USA, Germany and France) are often the least ecological in action. There is an inverse ratio between green rhetoric and sound green practice. Much of Africa and Asia has a tiny environmental impact per capita

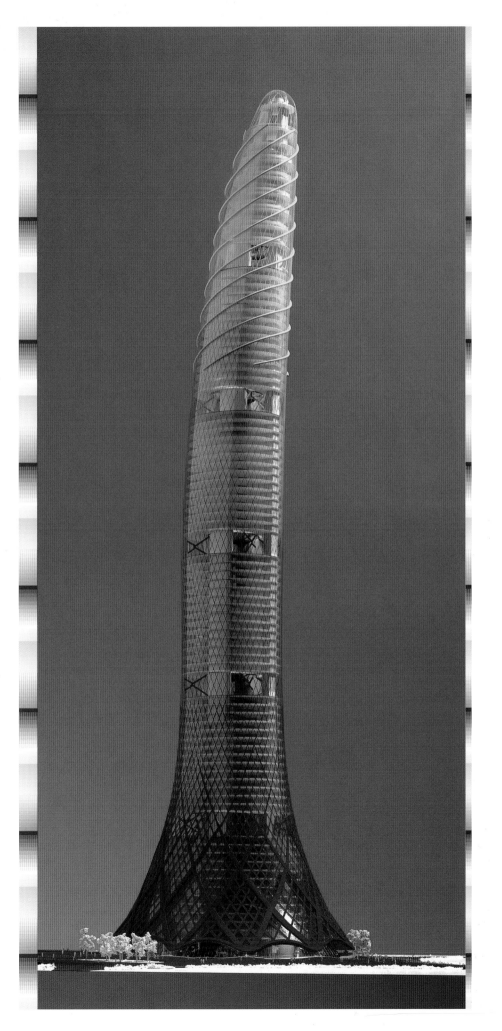

The close of
the century
witnessed a
fascinating
blend of
building
design,
known as
eco-tech
or eco-cool,
that embraced
precision
engineering,
computing
and ecology.

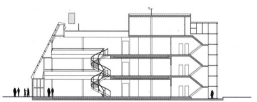

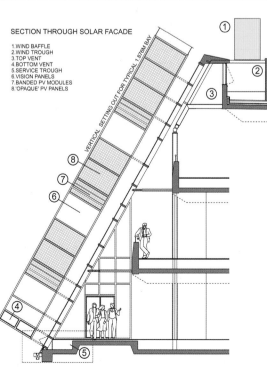

SECTION THROUGH SOLAR FACADE

1.WIND BAFFLE
2.WIND TROUGH
3.TOP VENT
4.BOTTOM VENT
5.SERVICE TROUGH
6.VISION PANELS
7.BANDED PV MODULES
8.'OPAQUE' PV PANELS

① ② ③ ④ ⑤ ⑥ ⑦ ⑧

VERTICAL SETTING OUT FOR TYPICAL 1.875M BAY

Opposite
Studio E Architects, Doxford
Solar Office, Sunderland, 1998.
With health emerging as the
'wild card' of sustainability,
buildings such as the Doxford
Solar Office are helping to
promote the personal health
and productivity of employees
as well as the wider global
health of the population.

Above
In cities such as San Francisco
the immediacy of environ-
mental issues is brought home
by pollution. For it threatens
not only San Francisco's idyllic
natural climate and setting but
also, ultimately, its prosperity
which rests on the city's ability
to attract tourists in the short
term and companies and
investors in the long term.

compared to the West and their examples of green design are rarely to be found in the growing genre of books and journals that deal with sustainability. As a general statement, the spiritual approach to green design is found in the underdeveloped world and the low-energy, high-material approach in the developed.

Both history and geography provide valuable lessons which allow today's practice to be set in a wider social and cultural context. Sustainability has been a recurring challenge for mankind since men and women began to settle the surface of the earth. Being nomadic relieved the human race of a duty of care towards the land – as soon as they formed villages they could not hide from the environmental consequences of physical development. These consequences expressed themselves in a variety of ways: pollution, scarcity of resources and sickness. Health has been a perennial problem as towns have grown – illness arguably has been a greater motor of sustainability than energy. It was the search for healthy living that introduced refuse control in classical cities, that ensured open space existed in medieval towns, that regulated the use of building materials, controlled the extraction and use of water, and laid down a

network of drains in countless settlements from the Renaissance onwards. This legacy is apparent in the countless building acts and model by-laws of the 19th century. What is obvious is that it was not low-energy design or the need to preserve biodiversity or protect environmental resources that structured early European settlements, but public health. And today it is health – both global and personal – which is emerging as the 'wild card' of sustainability. The future promises a new contract between global energy use and health, and in this equation buildings and cities will play a crucial role.

One lesson of history is that the constraint on sustainable development is rarely resource scarcity. What limits human action is waste and its consequences – the 'sink', not lack of energy and other resources, tends to curtail the system. The limits to prosperity in cities like London or Hong Kong are not resource constraints but pollution ones. And with pollution health goes and disease comes. Urban road pollution is now the second biggest killer in Europe, accounting for 60,000 deaths a year from lung cancer, heart disease and bronchitis.[2] Road traffic and urban exhaust air from buildings kill more people than smoking. Sink limits threaten the human race more insidiously than resource limits. And at the root of pollution lies consumption – that insidious search for consumer happiness promoted by countless global multinationals.

With this change in emphasis comes a clear new agenda for building design. Architecture, which accounts for roughly half of all resource consumption in the world (materials, energy, water and the loss of fertile agricultural land), has to come to terms with the fact that the wastes from buildings are busy polluting the planet and destroying the health of people. What is at risk here is the health and wellbeing not only of people in buildings but also of cities, and with this the viability of human civilisation itself.

Consumption is itself a problem. We now consume more per capita than ever before – consumer goods, cars and space itself. Excess consumption is often expressed in excess architectural display, in exaggerated High Tech posturing and over-ambitious space and comfort levels. Buildings are fashion accessories – the backcloth to commercial and private lives. Within our homes we create space for gadgets rather than people, we fill our offices with computers, our airports with shops. So whereas buildings consume half of all environmental resources, they either house the space where the other half is consumed or form the destination for the essential journeys required for human connection. As a system, cities are the focus of resource use and pollution – buildings are an ecology of global impacts which we are only beginning to understand.

Above
Michael Hopkins and Partners, University of Nottingham Jubilee Campus, 1999. Built on the site of a former derelict bicycle factory, this innovative green campus has a newly created lake as its centrepiece. This provides a natural habitat for wildlife and aquatic species which combine to create an ecologically balanced park. Cool air is also picked up from the lake's surface and is used to ventilate the campus's atrium-link spaces. Three of the main faculty buildings incorporate state-of-the-art energy-saving technologies funded by an EU grant. A prefabricated Western Red Cedar 'breathing wall' was specially developed for the project which incorporates a pulped-paper insulation system.

Green: the Search for an Earthly Paradise

In a world of universal space and increasingly standardised values, sustainability offers a chance to develop specific place-related design. If green is taken as representing a sympathetic approach to culture as well as climate, then sustainable architecture will emerge as a significant life-enhancing force. There is not one design culture (that is, late Modern Western) but a complex web of cultural diversity even within a single country, let alone the world. There is also not one climate to be responded to via universal air-conditioning and standardised building footprints. Sustainability breaks the monopoly of both Western cultural primacy and High Tech architectural solutions. Hence the resistance in the USA to any serious commitment to sustainability and the avoidance in the UK of significant mention of sustainable design in the Egan proposals.

Sustainability is deeply subversive politically. There may be no other environmental course than to become sustainable: civilisation requires to rethink more than two centuries of Western industrial philosophy. The forces which have led to universally placeless cities with their ubiquitous shopping malls, suburban estates, business parks, airports, etc are challenged by the green movement. 'Swampy' may stop a stretch of road building but the Brundtland definition of sustainable development (adopted by the UN and 183 world governments at the Rio summit in 1992) will make even the most measured architect into a Swampy.

The UN Kyoto Conference on Climate Change (1998) and the World Climate Change Conference at The Hague (2000) threatened to break the monopoly of universal architectural solutions as promulgated by big Western design practices. Buildings will no longer be the same again, and in time, neither will cities. Carbon quotas and emissions targets mean we will have to burn less fossil fuel – in our cars, industry and, most importantly, our buildings. The loss of depth of place, time and function will disappear: cities will again become identifiable places based upon a synthesis of cultural and environmental values.

There is no tenable argument which can separate environmental action from cultural action. Place is a statement about attitude to geography, history and resources. Placelessness (the prevalent 20th-century mode of development) was indifferent to all three. To

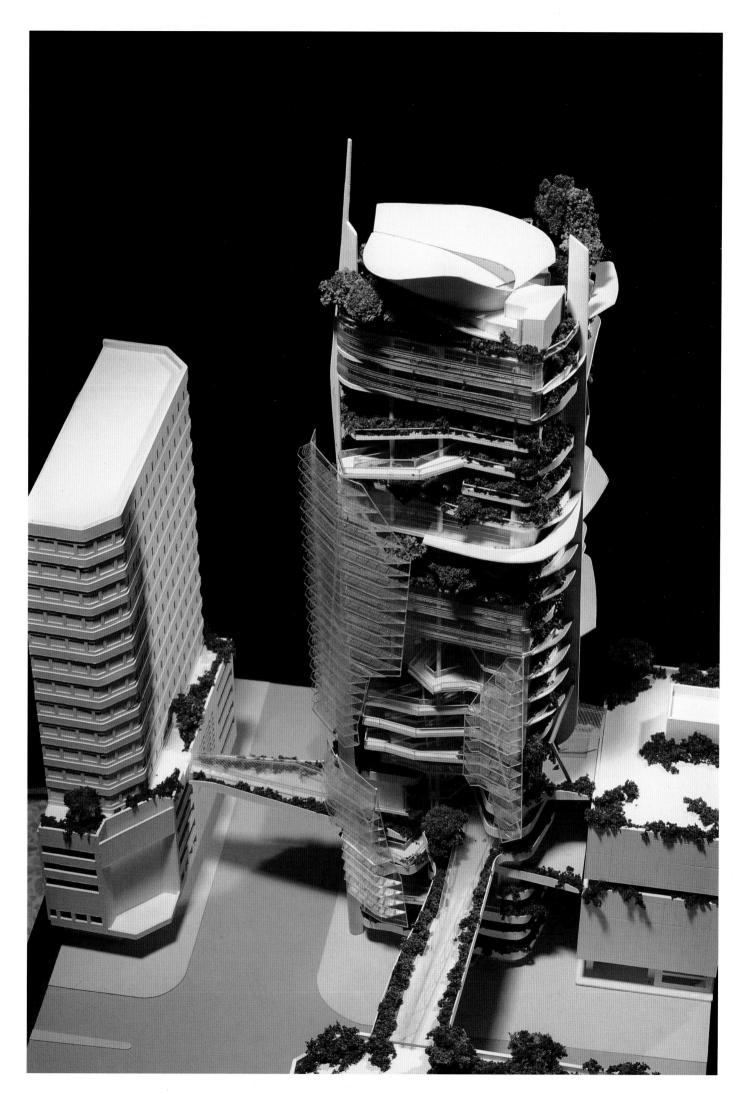

Previous page
Ken Yeang, EDITT Tower,
competition design 1998.
Intended to be built as an
exposition building in
Singapore, this project was
designed to explore an
ecological approach to tower
design in an urban area with
a devastated ecosystem. The
inorganicness of the current
site was to be addressed
through substantial planting
on the facades and vegetated
terracing.

Above
Feilden Clegg Bradley
Architects, Building Research
Establishment Office, Watford,
1996. This award-winning
office building was designed
as part of the Future Project,
a collaboration between the
Building Research
Establishment and industry
to investigate the parameters
of healthy, low-energy work
places for the 21st century.
As well as setting stringent
energy targets of 30 per cent
less than current best
practice, its brief called for
a landmark building with high
architectural standards.

meet new CO_2 targets we need to value fossil fuels as scarce and diminishing resources, and we need to exploit renewable energy sources (sun, wind, biomass). We need to develop new technologies and new solutions to building programmes. Since each place is different (resources, climate, exposure) building solutions will need to differentiate themselves more effectively than in the past. This means selecting more appropriate technologies, using the best, not cheapest, method of construction, employing life-cycle assessment, seeking out local sources of energy and materials, employing local building skills and know-how.

But differentiation is not just a question of new futures. It is about valuing old pasts. The vernacular was the evolution of patterns of building best suited to local conditions. Inefficient solutions became extinct over time, leaving only the fittest to survive. Old towns, whether in Asia, Africa or Europe, are reminders of how to build when materials are scarce; labour is valued for its workmanship (as against speed); resources of energy, food and water are locally sourced. The Aga Khan Awards for Architecture are among the few that give recognition to the past as informing the future. Sustainable design needs to recognise the lessons of cities which grew up in periods of

scarcity – lessons we need to relearn for the resource-hungry future. And it is not only a matter of construction – such lessons extend to the whole ecosystem of cities with their patterns of recycling, reuse and renewal.

Particular places, whether vernacular or designed, are valued for the meanings they carry. Social meaning allows towns and their buildings to be cherished, but in our multicultural society meaning in its broader sense has to have wide appeal. Its roots are many and varied, and much depends upon cultural conditioning. What architects value (tectonics, materiality, transparency, etc) may not be the same as what is valued by society at large. You have only to visit a McDonald's hamburger bar to see the mismatch between professional and public taste. Sustainability offers the chance to unify values around common environmental goals, bringing shared agendas back on to the architectural stage.

For this to happen we need to look beyond low-energy design as the panacea for sustainability. Low-energy buildings can produce dull, culturally impoverished architecture. True sustainable design takes on board the full complexity of ecology with its life-enhancing agenda. Nature uses the minimum of resources to create the maximum of richness and beauty, employing full recycling in the process. Western man, on the other hand, uses the maximum of resources to build cities of minimum richness and beauty, employing less than 10 per cent of recycling in the process. Man and nature urgently need to get their two systems together. When this happens (and this needs to be our goal for the 21st century) our mature-world cities will begin to approach the complexity and beauty of rainforests or coral reefs. There will be layers of interaction, with each system using the wastes of lower orders to create richness, beauty and self-sufficiency. The spiral of social, cultural and architectural ambition will be upwards, not downwards as at present. What will drive this spiral will be the fresh currents of sustainable imperative which, like the Gulf Stream, derive ultimately from the life force of the sun. Our old divisions between town and country, man and nature, ecology and culture will be broken. Architecture will at last be free of the tyranny of exploitative modernism: we will have in sight a new Earthly Paradise

Unsustainable Biblical Origins

It could be argued that Christian philosophy helped sow the seeds of anti-environmentalism in much of the Western world. The Bible is full of references to control, order and dominance of the natural world. Man's role in life was to subdue the earth (Genesis 1.28) and to rule over the garden (Genesis 2.15). What the Bible describes as mankind's 'dominion over fish ... fowl ... and every creeping thing'[3] led inevitably to an ethic of dominance. Our cities are a direct consequence of biblical unsustainability. The Christian foundation upon which Western society is built had an unfortunate tendency to place man apart from the natural order. By way of contrast, Eastern religions integrate mankind into a global ecological system. Such integration is not only physical but, more importantly, is also spiritual. The worldliness of Christianity – the call to multiply, exploit and prosper – has become in many aspects the international order of big business. It is the motor of stock exchanges from Tokyo to Lima, the basis upon which companies conduct their business and governments manage resources. Inevitably it is the basis, too, for cities and the countless buildings which, in their subtle variety, still express the Christian exploitative ideal.

UN definition of 'Sustainable Development' coined in 1987 by Gro Harlem Brundtland – a woman whose words have changed the course of history. The 'he-ness' of the Bible has been usurped by the 'she-ness' of sustainability. Brundtland followed in the steps of other prominent female environmentalists: Rachel Carson (*Silent Spring*), Barbara Ward who first coined the phrase 'sustainable development', and Donella Meadows of the Club of Rome (*Limits to Growth*).

The relationship between man and nature is more organic than cerebral. Though intellectual abstraction is a necessary component of human thought, the general attitude to the natural world is vital, immediate and revolves around the question of survival. However, though the outer face of nature appears increasingly hostile and unpredictable, the human condition also assigns a meaning beyond dependency for life to the environment. This search for deeper insight is

Our building technology has become leaner, more efficient and better integrated. It has allowed greater efficiency to be achieved in terms of energy use, construction output per man (or woman) and internal space per unit of structural resource.

The means by which dominance over nature has been achieved is largely facilitated by science and technology, and to an increasing extent by design. Both are at the centre of architectural practice. Our building technology has become leaner, more efficient and better integrated. It has allowed greater efficiency to be achieved in terms of energy use, construction output per man (or woman) and internal space per unit of structural resource. These objective gains have, however, failed to address the other reality – that which is behind the rational and underlies the scientific. The inner life, not only of people but of cities, has suffered. In effect we have lost sight of the building as a living thing. Our modern ugly cities with their pollution and stress are a kind of illness that reflects not only global environmental sickness but also a wider crisis in the human condition.

At the root of much green thinking lies an attempt to confront these issues and to provide a better balance between man and nature. Conceptually, sustainability reverses biblical teaching. It seeks not dominion over God's creation but gentle guardianship of the earth's bounteous resources. The human race is not apart from the global system but is integrated into it via the discipline of ecology – human, social and environmental. This is the basis of the

interpreted differently according to culture or religion. Though all people depend upon nature for sustenance, varying cultural constructions are assigned to ecology around the world. For example, Jesus equated God with nature – the Christian position has always been that beyond nature is the hand of a superior force over which mankind has guardianship. Christians looked through nature at God and in the process gave themselves dominion over all living things. GM crops, the BSE crisis, cloning and climate change all demonstrate the folly of this position.

The Greeks, on the other hand, looked through the gods at nature. The role of the gods was to express natural laws and to be go-betweens for the human race. Classicism celebrated nature not as a natural or primeval force, but as an object of harmony and beauty. Ecology was reduced to cult objects. Eastern religions adopt a quite different interpretation to that of either the Christian or the classical world. The Buddhist position treats nature as art, creating illusion in, and distorting, the natural world. There are no deep messages here – the human mind transcends the tertiary reality of nature.[4] Buddhist philosophy is a contract between man and God, acted out, with nature given a sublime role as a tranquil setting for meditation. There is a interdependence between mankind and the world at large – an inner and outer harmony which places nature within a bigger cosmic order. The Taoist position is again quite different: here there is an

Above
Santiago Calatrava, Sondica Airport, Bilbao, Spain, 2000. The way architecture is viewed is a key to the way buildings are designed. In contrast to Richard Rogers who finds analogies in nature, Calatrava uses the eye as a model of perpetual adaption to different conditions within a unified whole.

Opposite
Foster and Partners, SwissRe London headquarters, 1999. Designed for a leading firm of reinsurers on the site of the Baltic Exchange in the City of London, the office tower is conceived to be environmentally responsible; it makes particularly effective use of natural ventilation and light. With its unusual curved form standing out on London's skyline it is also intended, in Lord Foster's words, 'to be socially, technically, architecturally and spatially radical'.

aesthetic, almost stoical, appreciation of nature. The natural world is not the ultimate reality but prepares mankind for the eternal beauty of the afterlife. Nature is framed, captured, manicured and brought indoors in idealised form.

In old shamanic religions, the shaman had a special role to act as an intermediary between the present and past spirits of people, places and plants. He had powers to heal people and the environment. There were often both special places and special plants – the cultural heritage was a blend of man-made and natural features. From these grew cultural and social constructs which placed nature within the human condition – collective knowledge was essentially ecological in spirit.[5]

These general interpretations of different religions help to explain the paradox of modern attitudes to nature. There is no universal view, but a series of distinct cultural translations. As a consequence one cannot expect a single global reading of the ecological crisis – all peoples interpret the changing climatic and natural reality in a different fashion. Architecture, especially green architecture, is necessarily influenced by religious, social and cultural factors. There is no ecumenical green movement – merely a range of responses to the overriding agendas of sustainability and global warming.

We need to bring into focus the delightful and unexpected responses to current environmental problems around the world. Only a global view will counter the perception that there is a ubiquitous sustainable style irrespective of custom, climate, culture or place.

How we see our buildings is central to how we design them. Richard Rogers talks about an architecture of responsiveness, of buildings modelled upon the complexity and changeability of natural organisms. He cites birds and chameleons as useful models. Santiago Calatrava, on the other hand, uses the eye as an example of perpetual adaptation to different conditions within a unified whole. Louis Kahn, in similar spiritual mood, asked the brick what it most wanted to be and it answered 'an arch'. If we ask a piece of land what it wants to be it will not answer 'a city'. If we ask a flood plain it will not reply 'a housing estate'. Our task is to go beyond the rational – to seek an architecture which is a living thing, which enriches life at many levels and understands a few ecological truths.

Sick buildings and inefficient building types are a form of illness.[6] Their ugliness is an expression of suffering which affects everybody. The American poet Thomas Moore said that buildings are bound to us as another species. They are a kind of living presence; a member of the family, like our pets. Since we spend at least 80 per cent of our lives in buildings their impact upon human life is enormous. Our health, our souls and

our memories are fashioned by them. In Jungian psychology buildings only animate our life if they have anima – an inner personality. Without anima all is rational, cool and sterile. Green thinking is a way of giving living presence back to our architecture. We may argue that the agenda is low-energy design but in reality architects like Bill Dunster, Ken Yeang and Norman Foster are seeking to confront the lost inner world of architectural space.

How Many Planets Does the Human Race Need?

At present levels of consumption, the human species requires about three Earths to sustain itself. We are exceeding the carrying capacity of natural systems by a factor of three generally, six in the West and one or one and a half in Africa. The areas of resource stress are in fossil fuels, in agricultural land, in the availability of clean drinking water, in hardwood products, in fish and, most importantly, in terms of the global climate. As we modify the Earth to meet human need there is a loss of species, genetic diversity and virgin habitats. The planet is becoming an enormous farm to support rapidly growing cities. Ecological strain is evident everywhere and the human race readily accepts the global extinction of perhaps 4,000 species a year in order to streamline the Earth into a production line to support its own activities. In this we have assumed godlike qualities as Genesis predicted.

If other planets were available the problem would not be so great. As it is, we are alone in the universe (at least in terms of nearby potential habitation) and cannot yet begin to exploit the resources elsewhere. Though Mars and Jupiter have enormous resources, the embodied energy involved in extracting them is prohibitive. So we consume at a factor of exhaustion that approaches 3:1 and face the prospect of our own extinction in a few hundred years. Unless, that is, we can manage our way out of a crisis – manage in the sense of addressing a broad spectrum of human activities including design.

The two areas of imminent resource stress – fossil fuels and climate instability – are both directly influenced by decisions made by architects. Buildings consume half of all fossil-fuel energy and the totality of cities consume three-quarters. Our decisions as building designers and city makers are crucial to the survival not just of mankind, but of natural systems generally. It is said that 80 per cent of global photosynthesis now goes to supporting *Homo sapiens* – like the dinosaurs we are dominant, aggressive and at the top of all food chains. Mankind holds in its hands not only its own destiny but also that of nature's rich inheritance. Mankind has been given guardianship of a living system and architects need to realise that they shape all life through their designs, not only human habitats. *Δ*

Notes
1. Richard Rogers, BBC Reith Lectures, 1995. See also Ivor Prinsloo, *Architecture: A Modern View*, Thames and Hudson (London), 1991, p 58 where Rogers cites the adaptability of the chameleon.
2. Reported on 'Today', BBC Radio 4, 14 August 2000.
3. Genesis 1.26.
4. John B Noss, *Man's Religions*, Macmillan (London), third edition, 1967, p 32.
5. John B Noss; here I am indebted to Chrisna du Plessis for recent guidance.
6. Here I am indebted to Professor Freeman Chan for his paper delivered at the Chinese University of Hong Kong, 16 September 2000.

Design Challenge of
Sustainability

Sustainability is currently the most pressing, complex and challenging agenda facing architects. The ever-expanding urban population of the globe has meant that over the last decade it has moved on from being a single concern, focused largely on global warming, to one where much wider issues of the environment and ecological health are at stake. Brian Edwards shows how this might be turned to positive effect, as sustainability comes to the fore as the only viable movement bridging the social purpose with the technological, and nature becomes the newest tool in the design process.

The evidence that global warming exists is overwhelming. Science has established beyond doubt the correlation between burning fossil fuels and planetary warming. More recent evidence shows that other activities of mankind are accelerating the rise in global temperatures. These include the destruction of rainforests (mainly to supply the world's construction industry), waste and the associated release of methane gases. Global warming is an uncomfortable fact for politicians, designers, the construction industry and the human race. It is also an uncomfortable reality for many other global species who see their habitats destroyed by forest clearing, sea-level rise and desertification. We not only place ourselves under threat; the whole ecosystem is stressed by global warming.

But global warming is only part of the challenge. We are witnessing a major drift to cities by the human population. The year 2000 marked the first time in mankind's history that the urban population exceeded the rural one. Of our global population of six billion, more people now live in cities than in the countryside. This not only entails an intensification of urban problems (pollution, space, crowding and resource stress) but also raises expectations of an enhanced lifestyle. With this go the personal goals of air conditioning, car and energy-consuming gadgets of various kinds. As the human species becomes more urban we consume more and pollute more. This, as Richard Rogers pointed out in his Reith lectures in 1996, shifts the emphasis from buildings to urban design, and from simple choices (such as energy) to complex ones (such as ecology). The environment is increasingly stressed by mankind's success and population growth. It is anticipated that by 2050 the global human population will be 10 billion. By then there may well be more humans than all the other large mammals put together.

The stresses imposed by such growth touch upon resources and waste. The big question for global ecologists today is whether human success as a species will be constrained by resource scarcity or pollution. Will waste succeed in limiting growth in consumption more effectively than the inability to secure ever more resources? With two per cent global economic growth per year (the World Trade Organization's prediction) and a population of 10 billion, it is easy to see that in 50 years the overall environmental impact of the human population will be 10 times what it is today (at compound interest). This impact will be felt primarily in cities and will stress the existing building stock as much as it will stress people. Today's buildings will need to accommodate the future scarcity of resources. Pollution and the intensified pressure on space that will result from the mushrooming human population will focus upon an ever smaller geographical area: the city.

Over the past decade we have moved from a concern for global warming, with its associated international agreements (Rio, Kyoto), to a wider concern for the state of cities, the environment and ecological health. This shift is central to the notion of sustainable development. Sustainability is intellectually more interesting, professionally more challenging and in design terms more demanding than any other agenda. It has emerged as the new cutting edge in science, the basis for innovative new technologies and design approaches, the fresh paradigm for social equity and the lens through which we view human development. Sustainability is the concern of the best thinkers of our age – it can be traced as an underlying theme in the Harry Potter books, in Seamus Heaney's reinterpretation of Beowulf, in Peter Hall's rewriting of urban history. For many of the world's best architects (Piano, Yeang, Foster) it is the challenge of our age – the first unifying basis for a new architecture since Le Corbusier's *Towards a New Architecture* was published in 1927.

> What is often ignored in architectural circles is the way sustainable development as a concept bridges two central agendas of building design: technology and social purpose.

What is often ignored in architectural circles is the way sustainable development as a concept bridges two central agendas of building design: technology and social purpose. Many recent movements in architecture have played to only one side of the equation. High Tech was high architecture with little social justification. Community architecture ignored the power of technology to solve human problems. But sustainability brings the two camps together: it not only reinvigorates architecture, it gives fresh moral validity to the creation of human settlements. And here lies the basis of a new

Opposite
View of Sydney from the air, 2000. From above, the incredible density of the city is apparent. With more people living in urban areas than rural ones, urban problems are intensifying. This brings all the associated symptoms of poor housing, traffic congestion and pollution. On a global scale, the urbanisation of society also acts as a catalyst to mass consumerism, with city life driving up life-style expectations.

Above top: left to right
Edward Cullinan Architects,
Millennium School, Greenwich,
London, 2001. As well as being
ecologically compatible, this
sustainably responsive design
for a primary school on the
Greenwich Peninsula is
intended to bring greater
social wellbeing to the local
community.

Above bottom: left & right
Penoyre & Prasad Architects,
The Millennium Centre,
Eastbrookend Country Park,
Dagenham, 1997. Designed for
a country park reclaimed after
a century of mineral extraction
and landfill, the building was
explicitly conceived to
contribute to the greening of
its immediate area. It was
designed to give visitors the
key to understanding local
ecology and natural history.

flowering of architectural talent after the dark ages of much of the 20th century. The marriage of technology and social sustainability brings a need to understand materials and their details on the one hand, and the agents of community wellbeing (and hence urban design) on the other. This refiguring of the architectural challenge touches base on questions of local building traditions, of fresh patterns of streets and buildings, whilst also seeking greater ecological compatibility and social wellbeing. Many consequences flow from the challenge of fashioning more sustainable cities and buildings. For example, what should the relationship be between town and country – are green belts really necessary when urban transport is linear rather than circular? What are the new balances required of ecological design – is energy going to dominate green architecture at the expense of other sustainable considerations? Since buildings are enormous resource-consumers (about 50 per cent of energy, water, materials and global agricultural land) should one not design buildings as ecosystems with inputs and outputs joined in recycling loops? Should architecture not also address social cohesion, allowing our buildings to unify peoples rather than divide them? Is a new approach needed to urban design: are cities not merely big buildings unified by glazed galleries, gardens and multifunctioning towers?

It is time to take stock of where green architecture is going. Early pioneers (Fuller, Brundtland, the Vales) emphasised the energy dimension in sustainability. It remains a primary concern because of accelerating levels of global carbon emissions. But does low-energy design on its own produce great architecture? There is little evidence to link high aesthetics to energy conservation – in fact, the contrary is often the case. It is only when the full picture of ecological design is addressed that a rich, complex and beautiful architecture emerges. Future Systems' buildings and the recent work of Foster's office are landmarks to sustainable – not low energy – design. These and the works of other practices may whistle to the tune of global warming but in reality they are producing (to use Ken Yeang's term) bioclimatic, ecologically responsive buildings. And in the process they are developing new exciting technologies, some of which are borrowed from other industries. These buildings also closely address human needs, both physical and psychological. They are structures that express social sustainability at the level of human health, productivity and wellbeing. Foster's High Tech, breathing buildings are almost lungs in which people dwell. The search for a responsive environment is as much driven by the human appetite for spiritual uplift as it is by technological innovation. Social, ecological and cultural sustainability will be the measures for tomorrow's buildings.

The human drift to cities is accompanied by two further consequences for sustainable design. The human race now spends 80 per cent of its time indoors –

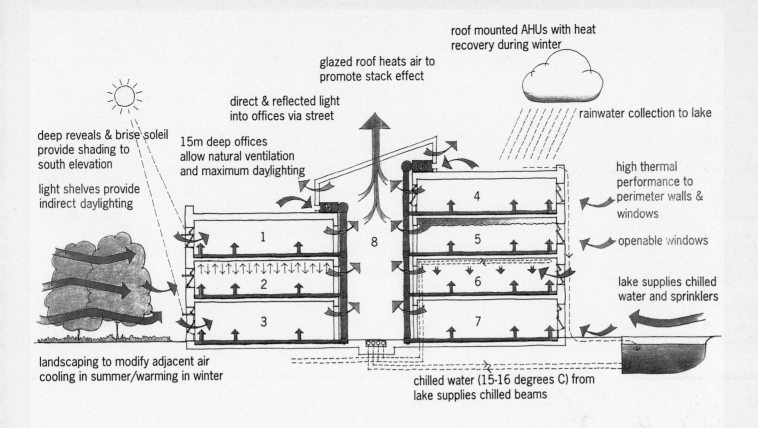

roof mounted AHUs with heat recovery during winter

glazed roof heats air to promote stack effect

direct & reflected light into offices via street

rainwater collection to lake

deep reveals & brise soleil provide shading to south elevation

15m deep offices allow natural ventilation and maximum daylighting

light shelves provide indirect daylighting

high thermal performance to perimeter walls & windows

openable windows

lake supplies chilled water and sprinklers

landscaping to modify adjacent air cooling in summer/warming in winter

chilled water (15-16 degrees C) from lake supplies chilled beams

Above
Fitzroy Robinson, Barclaycard HQ, Northampton, 1996. Creating a healthy responsive environment for staff is often more important to companies than keeping energy costs down.

60 years in a lifetime. The human habitat is essentially an interior. The environments we create affect us in terms of our physical and mental health. Sustainability is the key to how an architecture of interior occupation can be fashioned to support healthy and productive life styles. Recent research suggests that green buildings enhance working performance and social harmony. A productive, positive and healthy work force is more important to a typical company than the money saved in the lower utility bills of green design. When a company such as Barclaycard spends 50 per cent of its total outgoings on labour costs and two per cent on energy bills, it makes sense to provide healthy responsive working spaces for staff rather than focus on the single issue of low-energy design. The same is true of green schools and green hospitals, which enhance performance in many subtle ways (teachers are absent less often, better exam results, patients heal faster). These wider social benefits are beginning to be brought into clearer focus as the millennium unfolds. They represent the fusion of a solid technological base, social sustainability, productivity and social cohesion based on healthy life styles rather than the usual welfare rights and employment. For architects, too, the recognition of a social dimension to sustainability allows buildings to address issues beyond that of low-energy design.

Green: Nature as Guide

Different designers have learnt to employ nature's order in their own fashion, from Future Systems' exploitation of biomimicry, to Foster's approach which is more based on ecological systems, to Yeang's adoption of termite-tower principles of natural ventilation. However, as a design discipline nature is not without problems. It lacks a technological base and its outputs are rarely socially benign. Nevertheless, by blending technology and ecology it is possible to generate buildings and cities with reduced environmental impact by adopting the concept of vertically spiralling life-cycle loops. The concept offers architects a new tool in their search for less damaging construction.

Nature not only recycles; it moves upwards towards even greater complexity and beauty as the scale of complexity increases. It seems to have an inbuilt motor of diversity. It shuns repeats, cloning and the mindless search for perfect duplication which is mankind's preference. In this, nature offers a model for new city forms and fresh building typologies. Somehow we have to bring the beauty, richness and social diversity of coral reefs and rainforests to bear upon human creations.

Learning from nature entails using ecology in quite distinct ways. One has to remember that nature is not neutral – it has its own laws and methods of working. Darwin helped to discover the keys to the genesis of species and their interdependence within habitats. Others have unravelled the genetic codes to life itself. We are masters of this knowledge, but too rarely bring the principles to bear on architectural design. Our cities are dying just like the coral reefs – pollution, global warming and tourism ultimately kill anything that is delicate and beautiful.

How, then, can nature be our guide? Five quite distinctive potentials can be postulated.

1. Learning from nature. This was Ian McHarg's clarion call in his remarkable book of the same name, published in 1970. Nature has patterns and orders of interdependence which can be used to design buildings. Ecological design is an attempt to put these systems into the linear, functional equations normally employed. Life-cycle assessment allows buildings to take on the characteristics of natural systems. An analogy can be drawn between buildings (species) and cities (habitats). Learning from nature encourages an appreciation of how these interact, in resource terms, with energy, water and materials going in, and waste, pollution and contamination coming out. In effect, we have an architectural ecosystem where the restraint is arguably more a sink limit than a resource one. And it is the sink limit that is destroying the world's coral reefs, not the scarcity of resource inputs. Here we have a warning from nature.

2. Using nature's models to inform. The structures employed in nature are well tested. The shapes, compositions, configurations and materials used in nature are enduring and sustainable. Foster's famous gherkin-shaped office tower for London is an obvious example of biomimicry. His debating hall for the Greater London Authority, which looks like a section of a lung, is another. In both cases nature's tried and tested models are adapted to provide a responsive life enhancing architecture. Rogers' citing of the chameleon as an example of a potential architecture whose skin changes according to weather and light is another. Others from Future Systems to Santiago Calatrava draw upon a repertoire of forms found in nature. One characteristic stands out – the avoidance of the right angle, of mechanical repetitive linear thought.

Top left and top right
Foster & Partners, Headquarters for Greater London Authority, 1999. Like Foster's SwissRe headquarters in London, with its well-known gherkin shape, this proposal for a new building for the GLA, currently under construction, can be seen as an example of successful biomimicry, taking the form of a section of a lung.

Centre right
The richness and complexity of form and colour in nature can provide paradigms as well as inspiration for architectural order.

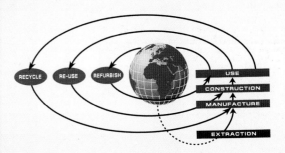

Above left
Eva Jiricna, Orangery, Prague Castle, 1999. Since its heyday in the 19th century, the glasshouse has been accommodating nature and ultimately celebrating it by making it its subject.

Above right
This British Steel diagram shows the degree to which life-cycle accounting has informed steel production.

3. Making nature explicit. Here architectural design brings nature into view, either inside or outside a building or directly in the construction materials employed. Nature is a source of tactile, visual and aural pleasure. When welcomed into buildings it has a practical purpose (to cleanse the air) and a spiritual one (to uplift the spirit, reduce stress and create harmony with the cosmos). The growth in atria has been accompanied by a corresponding increase in bringing nature indoors. Like the Victorian palm house, nature is now a commodity in commercial premises and almost a pet in the home. This has led some to speculate that our buildings are joined to us as another species – a kind of living entity which shares our life as a dynamic organism. Nature gives buildings their anima and hence, in Jungian terms, they are transformed from inanimate to living things.

4. Using nature for ecological accounting. All environmental assessment systems have an ecological basis though, because of the pressure of global warming, energy is normally the dominant theme. The Building Research Establishment Environmental Assessment Method (BREEAM) in the UK, Eco-quantum – auditing in The Netherlands and the Leadership in Energy and Design programme (LEED) in the USA employ an auditing system which treats the building as a habitat. Each subject, be it water, materials or energy, is a resource whose value is weighted according to its scarcity or damaging impact. The idea of nature-based accounting leads to the identification of 'indicators' which relieve designers of the task of assessing everything. These indicators are guides to good practice – they are selected according to building types and other conditions. They cast light on the health of the habitat – whether building or city.

5. Every species is a designer. Nature teaches us that all living creatures exercise design choices in some fashion. Nearly all options are limited by genetic inheritance – a particular ant can only build a particular type of ant hill – but it remains true that in nature all the parts contribute to the designed whole. The Bible claims that this is the hand of divine creation; Darwin, on the other hand, puts it down to natural selection. Either way, every living creature from high species to low is actively engaged in the search for richness, complexity and, ultimately, beauty itself. Applied to human ecology this means that everybody is a designer – every member of the human race is an architect since we all modify our environment and exercise design choices.

Certain understandings of global sustainable practice come from these classifications. It is clear that (2) is favoured by many architects for its formal possibilities. Nature is not understood as a system but is revered as a language of forms. Foster's recent exhibition at the Sainsbury Centre was peppered with the imagery of seashells, fish and trees. Future

The vernacular tradition is blended instinctively with aspects of social sustainability to forge a soft low-tech green architecture.

Top left
Fruto Vivas Architects with Buro Happold, Venezuelan Pavilion, Hanover Expo 2000. The Venezuelans responded to the Expo's theme 'Humankind-Nature-Technology' with a lightweight unfolding flower.

Top right
Squatter housing, Fez, Mexico. In shanty towns it is necessary for everyone to become a *bricoleur*, reusing whatever resources or materials are available and at hand.

Systems, too, have borrowed freely from ecological sources: flowers, plankton and starfish. Outside the UK other influences can be detected. Ken Yeang draws upon (1) in his search for a contemporary high-rise architecture that exploits natural currents upwards (for ventilation) and recycles wastes downwards (for composting). This is a philosophy which is system-based but still draws on a strong formal language of biomimicry.

Richard Rogers, on the other hand, makes frequent reference to (3) in both his buildings and in his city plans. Nature is allowed to colonise the interior spaces, the roof tops and the surrounding landscape. Rogers increasingly uses vegetation as another layer in his modification of the working environment. The justification is that of energy conservation but the effect is to uplift the spirit by making nature immediately visible. For Rogers, nature is both an aesthetic tool and a source of delight, necessary to humanise cities.

Looking further afield, the people-based architecture in parts of Asia, Africa and South America is analagous to everybody being a designer. Here, the vernacular tradition is blended instinctively with aspects of social

sustainability to forge a soft low-tech green architecture. You see it in the squatter camps of Mexico City (with admirable recycling but suspect public health), in South African townships away from official gaze. You see it, too, in the villages of the Brazilian rainforests where every house is different but each shares a common code of construction. These places are habitats in the true sense of the term, with humans one of many species present. Order is not the result of roads, regulations or sewers but of the logic of social space and local construction materials.

Of all the applications of nature none is more mechanistic than (4). Ecological accounting is a useful measure of impact but it rarely leads to great architecture. These assessment techniques started amongst the building scientists of the West and are now being applied universally. Few have social concerns bedded into their assessment tables and none weight beauty or complexity as desirable goals. In fact, the contrary is often the case – by subjecting designs to the rigour of carbon emission accounting it is possible to lose sight of the spiritual dimension. This is certainly true of BREEAM in the UK where resource-based assessment has led in the past to a reductionist architecture. So there needs to be balance in any eco-auditing system to ensure that the other benefits of nature remain visible.

Nature's Language	Architects/Organisation	Example
Learning from nature	Fielden Clegg Bradley	Building Research Establishment Office, Watford
	ECD	Slimbridge Visitor Centre, Gloucestershire
	Thomas Herzog	German Pavilion, Hanover Expo
	Lucien Kroll	Ecolonia, Aalphen, Holland
Using nature's models to inform	Norman Foster	SwissRe Building, London
	Future Systems	Media Centre, Lord's Cricket Ground, London
	Santiago Calatrava	Sondica Airport, Bilbao, Spain
	Ken Yeang	Shanghai Armoury Tower, Pudong
	Chetwood Associates	Sainsburys, Greenwich, London
Making nature explicit	Richard Rogers	Daimler Benz Building, Berlin
	Andrew Wright	Holy Island Retreat, Scotland
	Michael Hopkins	Jubilee Campus, University of Nottingham
	Ted Cullinan	Hooke Park, Dorset
Using nature for ecological accounting	Novem, The Netherlands	Eco-auditing system
	Building Research Establishment, UK	BREEAM, Schools Enviromental Assessment Method
	Department of the Environment, Transport and the Regions, UK	'Opportunities for Change'
	Kyoto Protocol, Japan	Carbon trading
	Green Buildings Council, USA	LEED
Every species is a designer	Shaman	Rural village plans
	Vernacular builders	Squatter housing
	Hunter-gatherers	Temporary jungle shelters
	Birds	Weaver-bird nests
	Insects	Termite towers

Health and Sustainability

Green buildings are frequently promoted for their healthy life styles. A low-energy design often entails forming environments which contribute via natural ventilation, daylight and the use of organic materials to less sick-building syndrome. The question of architectural health is a complex one: is physical or psychological health the key, and are the fluctuations in temperature that occur with more sustainable practices more in step with the natural world than the stereotypical environment of air conditioning? Many people who live or work in green buildings claim a 'feel good factor'. For others it is a 'forgiveness factor' because of excessive summertime heat and midwinter cold. In the natural world we adjust our environment

Right
Peter Foggo Associates, sketch of interior of Leeds City Office Park constructed for British Gas in 1995. This is one of the first speculative commercial office buildings to combine energy conservation with healthy working conditions. Designed to maximise on natural light in plan and elevation and saving on the use of artificial light, it also has solar light shades on the exterior which deflect light back into the centre of the offices. This affords adaptive work spaces for staff, who are able to control light levels with blinds and open windows.

Above and Opposite
Renzo Piano Building
Workshop, UNESCO Laboratory
and Workshop, Punta Nave,
Genoa, 1991. This was built by
Piano to house his own studio
and a UNESCO laboratory.
Positioned on a stepped slope,
it echoes the ancient terraces
of the Ligurian coast in its
interior and exterior structure.
Built entirely of glass with a
laminated wood frame, it looks
like one of the many
greenhouses scattered along
the Italian Riviera. Plants in
the building and on adjacent
terraces bring a special
contact with nature to the
laboratory and workshop.

and expectations to suit changing external conditions – extra clothes, more shelter, more logs in winter. The effect of this adjustment is physical, and to some extent psychological. In adjusting we are making a positive response and feel better.

The problem with modern environmentally sealed buildings is that the occupants cannot make these adjustments – the heater controls are fixed, the windows locked closed. Increasingly today, modification to living and working environments is needed to deal not with temperature difference but with mental stress. Levels of stress vary throughout the day in the work place but the building is often fixed and unforgiving. Buildings designed to sustainable principles, however, are more adaptive – you can open windows, move into pools of sunlight, touch plants in atria or window boxes, or simply sit in the cold to cool down. So as the stress levels of modern life rise you can adjust your own space to suit your psychological and physical needs. Green buildings are good for stress.

This argument could be employed at a global level. There are different conditions of external environment that are caused by natural cycles, and a further layer caused by mankind's activities. Green cities can absorb these fluctuations more effectively than highly engineered rigid structures can. The adaptive nature of sustainable design encourages the creation of a responsive world. Such responsiveness is essential in a future of higher temperatures, rainfall and pollution stress. Uncertainty cannot be countered by the certainties of old ways – high-tech design, air conditioning, mechanistic predictions. The global design and engineering community needs to rethink its technological assumptions – to find a better way of using the fruits of science. It will require architects to search deeper into their imaginations.

Health is emerging as the 'wild card' of sustainability. For a long time Western society has focused on energy but the relationship between this and health has led to some new understandings. Lack of affordable heat is a major cause of health-related illness in many poor housing estates in Europe and the USA. Excessive heat is a killer in parts of Asia, Africa and the Pacific Rim. We moderate our environment largely to produce healthy conditions, not to consume or save energy. If the global warming equation was set out in terms of its effect on health rather than energy a different picture would emerge. Carbon consumption could be set against benefits or harm to health which would allow a better understanding of the interactions with food production, water conservation, and energy use. Health is already emerging as the primary concern of UN agencies, especially those working in Africa. Famine, AIDS and a recurrence of tuberculosis as a major killer in the world mean that health and not

If oil and water help to define the differences in sustainable practices in the architectures of the world, there is a sense that the challenge of ecological design can combine the mechanistic strength of the West and the spiritual depth of the East.

energy is setting the agenda. Sustainable design needs not only to learn from nature but from health. Energy conservation is a subset of health; health is not a subset of energy consumption.

Is it Oil or Water that Matters?
The different regional perspectives on sustainability are well illustrated by the different nature of 'sink limits' in different parts of the world. In the industrialised West, air pollution is becoming a major constraint on development. In London, Paris, New York and Los Angeles poor air-quality poses a serious risk to public health – the EU estimates that air pollution from traffic is the second biggest killer in Europe, leading to 60,000 deaths a year from bronchitis and heart disease. In Africa, on the other hand, water pollution is the killer. Unsafe drinking water kills more people than AIDS and, according to the UN only a third of the population has clean water to drink. So whereas in the West the strategy for sustainable development focuses on energy conservation (and hence less air pollution), in much of Africa and Asia it revolves around water supply issues. And herein lies one of the

roots to sustainable diversity: energy and the corresponding equation of global-warming gases is abstract, scientific and mechanistic in its measures; water is wedded to the land and connects not with the rational but the spiritual world. Water is tactile, visible and in Africa and India it is directly related to health and agricultural productivity. The shamanic world is concerned with water not oil, and hence with the aesthetic and spiritual. No wonder water is increasingly seen as tomorrow's oil.

If oil and water help to define the differences in sustainable practices in the architectures of the world, there is a sense that the challenge of ecological design can combine the mechanistic strength of the West and the spiritual depth of the East. Even if society does not find itself limited by resource constraints, sink limits will drive design towards a more holistic agenda. Holistic in the sense of combining the priorities of energy and water conservation, of adopting life-cycle assessment as a measure of robustness in the choice of all materials, and in the integration of the rational and spiritual dimensions. And herein lies one of the seeds of architecture's renaissance. By relieving building design of its obsessive materiality, architecture can explore typologies and orders which learn from the two great traditions of cultural thought: Christianity and Islam. △

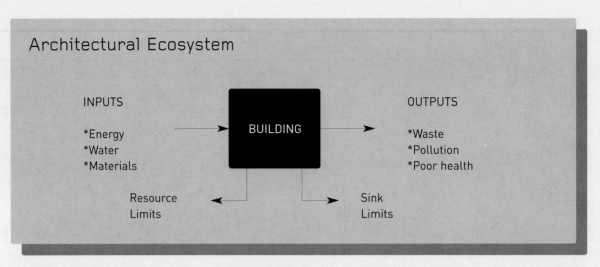

Architectural Ecosystem

INPUTS

*Energy
*Water
*Materials

BUILDING

OUTPUTS

*Waste
*Pollution
*Poor health

Resource
Limits

Sink
Limits

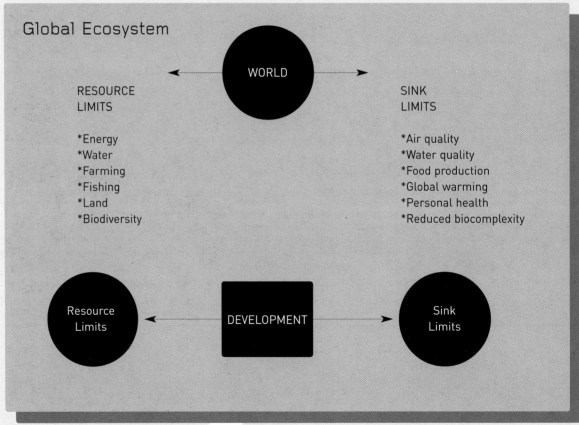

Global Ecosystem

WORLD

RESOURCE
LIMITS

*Energy
*Water
*Farming
*Fishing
*Land
*Biodiversity

SINK
LIMITS

*Air quality
*Water quality
*Food production
*Global warming
*Personal health
*Reduced biocomplexity

Resource
Limits

DEVELOPMENT

Sink
Limits

Global Resources	
Resource	**Building use**
Energy	50%
Water	42%
Materials (by bulk)	50%
Agricultural land loss	48%
Coral reef destruction	50% (indirect)

Global Pollution	
Pollution	**Building related**
Air quality (cities)	24%
Global warming gases	50%
Drinking water pollution	40%
Landfill waste	20%
CFCs/HCFCs	50%

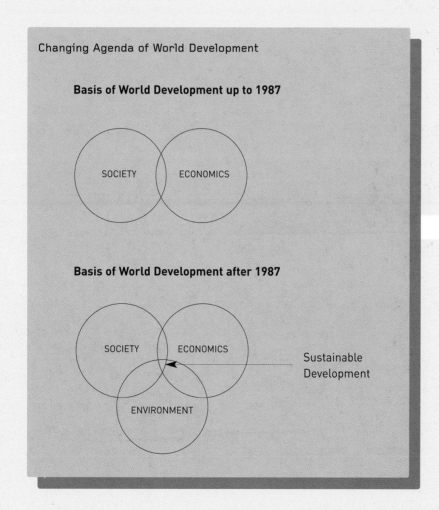

Changing Agenda of World Development

Basis of World Development up to 1987

SOCIETY ECONOMICS

Basis of World Development after 1987

SOCIETY ECONOMICS

ENVIRONMENT

Sustainable Development

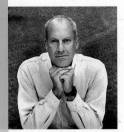

Lord Foster of Thames Bank

Green Questionnaire

What is your, or your practice's, definition of sustainable design?

Sustainable design means doing the most with the least means. 'Less is more' is, in ecological terms, exactly the same as the proverbial injunction, 'Waste not, want not'.

It is about ideally using passive architectural means to save energy – rather than relying on wasteful mechanical services, which use up dwindling supplies of nonrenewable fuel and produce pollution that contributes to global warming. But in the final analysis, sustainability is about good architecture. The better the quality of the architecture – and that includes the quality of thinking and ideas as much as the quality of the materials used – the longer the building will have a role, and in sustainability terms, longevity is a good thing. Obviously, if a building can be long-lasting and energy efficient, that is even better.

What are your key concerns as a designer interested in sustainability?

Sustainable architecture is not simply about individual buildings, but also our ever-expanding cities and their infrastructures. Unchecked urban sprawl is one of the chief problems facing the world today. As our cities grow horizontally rather than vertically, swallowing up more and more land, people are forced to travel greater distances between home and work. Mixed-use developments within cities can help to increase density, creating lively local communities that live, work and play in the same area. The Millennium Tower that we proposed in Tokyo takes a traditional horizontal city quarter – housing, shops, restaurants, cinemas, museums, sporting facilities, green spaces and public transport networks – and turns it on its side to create a supertall building with a multiplicity of uses. It would be over 800 metres high with 170 storeys – twice the height of anything so far built – and would house a community of up to 60,000 people. This is 20,000 more than the population of Monaco, already one of the densest cities in the world. Yet the building would occupy only 0.013 square kilometres of land compared to Monaco's 1.95 square kilometres. It would be a virtually self-

sufficient, fully self-sustaining community in the sky. Almost all the traffic would be internal. This sounds like future fantasy. But we have, now, all the means at our disposal to create such buildings.

How would you judge the success of a building in the 'green' age?

A 'green' building will use as little energy as possible and will make the most of the embodied energy required to build it. Ideally, a building should create its own energy by burning renewable fuels such as vegetable oil and harvesting solar energy. If possible it should create more energy than it uses so that it can provide energy to other buildings. The building should have a structure that allows for flexibility so that it will have a long life. We have already proved these concepts in the Reichstag – the new German parliament in Berlin.

In what way do you use nature as a guide?

We look to vernacular traditions that are specific to the area in which we are working. Very often there are rich architectural traditions that work with, and not against, nature which have been forgotten over time. In two projects in the Mediterranean we are using pergolas – large cable trellises covered with plants to provide natural shading and integrate the building visually within the landscape. In the American Air Museum at Duxford in Cambridgeshire and the Glass House at the National Botanic Garden of Wales near Cardiff, we partially buried the structures in the ground, again to integrate them within the landscape, but also to make passive use of the thermal mass of the soil to help save energy.

Our Chesa Futura in St Moritz in Switzerland uses timber construction, which makes environmental sense for a number of reasons. It is culturally sympathetic, reflecting local architectural traditions, and it contributes to the established ecology of felling older trees to facilitate forest regeneration. Furthermore, wood is an entirely renewable resource; it absorbs carbon dioxide during its growth cycle; and if indigenous timber is used, little or no energy is expended in its transportation.

Finally, in traditional towns and villages in Switzerland buildings are clustered tightly together rather than sprawling over the landscape. Chesa Futura is a reminder of the importance of building more intensely in existing urban concentrations to preserve the natural world. ∆

Above
Lord Foster of Thames Bank.

Opposite left
Model of Millenium Tower, Tokyo, 1989.

Opposite top right
Chesa Futura Apartments Project, St Moritz, 2000.

Opposite middle right
Exterior of Great Glass House, National Botanic Garden of Wales, 2000.

Opposite bottom
American Air Museum at Duxford, 1997.

Jan Kaplicky of Future Systems

Green Questionnaire

What is your, or your practice's, definition of sustainable design?

The major aspects of sustainable design are choice of materials and the performance of a building once it is built. Buildings have to be self-sufficient in energy – 80 per cent or more. It is even now possible to be selling energy back into the electricity grid overnight. Long-term performance, however, is very difficult to quantify. There is as yet no real unit of measurement. Energy also has to be considered in the construction of a building: how much will be consumed during construction and before that in the production of the materials. This also means that the quantity and weight of materials have to be given serious consideration for the first time. The fewer materials a building uses the greener it is – less resources and energy are used to produce it.

What are your key concerns as a designer interested in sustainability?

Materials, as I have suggested, are absolutely top priority. The impact sustainability is going to have on design, however, is going to be much more revolutionary. At the moment, people are trying to pretend that the need to produce sustainable architecture is going to have no effect on the form of buildings. It is like when the car was first invented and it imitated the form of the horse-drawn carriage. It took a certain amount of time for it to take on its own form. Rather than just being kosher, green architecture needs to find its own form. Airflow and cross ventilation will, for instance, have an important impact on the form of buildings.

How would you judge the success of a building in the 'green' age?

As yet there have been no truly green buildings built. The buildings that are currently being constructed aren't even prototypes for a 'green' age. They are only minor attempts at sustainability. The law as it stands doesn't give significant changes, especially in the US and UK. There is very little room for green architecture in architecture schools. An American lecturer at a well-known US school recently referred to it merely as fashion. It is evident that completely new thinking is required. The motorcar didn't happen until the engine existed. Intelligent buildings don't as yet exist.

In what way do you use 'nature' as a guide.

Nature can be used as a model at many different levels. For instance, termites' nests have two skins with natural ventilation. In between nature's structures also have a lightness not presently found in man-made constructions. They are far lighter in weight than those made by man and comparably far greater in strength. The thread in a spider's web, for instance, is twice as strong as steel. There is so much to learn from a more efficient use of materials. In general, organic forms are far more efficient than man's. Δ

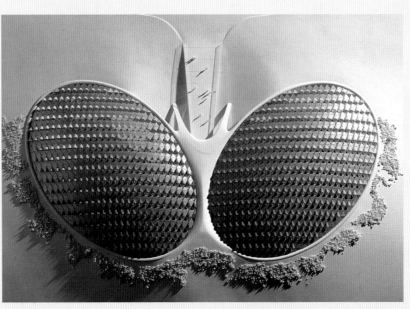

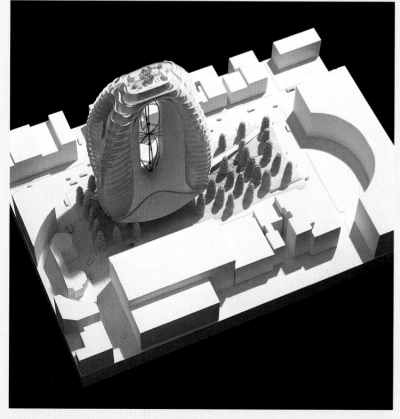

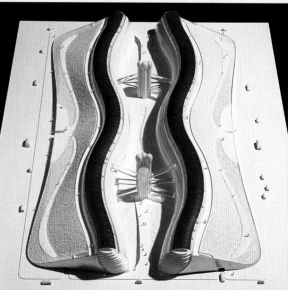

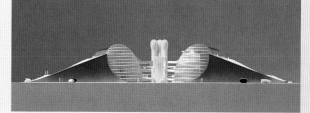

Lord Rogers of Riverside

Green Questionnaire

What is your, or your practice's, definition of sustainable design?

Sustainable design aims to meet present needs without compromising the stock of natural resources remaining for future generations. It must include a concern for the principles of social and economic sustainability as well as the specific concerns of the energy use and environmental impact of buildings and cities. The key issues are: low energy; loose fit; resource efficiency.

What are your key concerns as a designer interested in sustainability?

Buildings are responsible for 50 per cent of the world's generation of CO_2.

Richard Rogers Partnership has a long-standing concern with environmental performance, reflecting the personal interests of the directors. The practice sees issues of energy use and environmental impact as a critical part of the building and urban design process. True sustainability, in terms of building design, is dependent on maximum energy efficiency coupled with the use of replenishable materials. Specialist analysis and research inform design and encourage innovation in environmental systems and technologies.

RRP has pioneered the development of 'intelligent' buildings that can contribute substantially (up to 75 per cent) to reducing the running and maintenance costs during the life cycle of a building. Our aim is that the new building for the National Assembly for Wales in Cardiff will have zero CO_2 emission, for example.

The practice also has evolved an approach to civil, accessible and ecological urban design. The masterplans for Shanghai and for ParcBIT in Mallorca are key examples that demonstrate a strong ecological framework. Sustainable planning is a key feature of the practice's work, in particular the Greenwich Peninsula, where the practice produced a masterplan and redevelopment strategy for English Partnerships, including one of a handful of 'Millennium' villages that will encourage good sustainable design in the 21st century.

How would you judge the success of a building in the 'green' age?

The practice has an ongoing commitment to the development of 'intelligent' buildings that can contribute to a substantial reduction in the running and maintenance costs during the life cycle of a building.

Greater sustainability is achievable through:

- Intelligent design – harnessing the benefits and efficiencies of integrated passive environmental design through orientation, building form and organisation.

- The use of an intelligent building fabric – responsive facades can maximise natural daylight, optimise natural ventilation, control solar gain and loss.

- The appropriate use of materials – concern for the 'hidden' environmental costs of building materials (embodied energy and life-cycle issues), the benefits of transferring technology from other industries and the use of advanced, clean means of production.

- Intellectual capital – the analysis of the behaviour of buildings, application of CFD modelling and, especially, close collaboration with specialist consultants leads to the intelligent use of thermal mass, buffer zones, thermal flywheels, efficient airflows, etc.

In what way do you use nature as a guide?

Nature provides inspiration, information and analogy. ⌂

Above
Lord Rogers of Riverside

Right
Bordeaux Law Courts, France, 1998.

Opposite top left
Lloyd's Register of Shipping, 2000.

Opposite top right
88 Wood Street, London, 1999.

Opposite centre far right
Computer rendering by Hayes Davidson of Richard Rogers Partnership's National Assembly for Wales, due for completion in early 2003.

Opposite bottom and inset
Shanghai masterplan, 1992–94.

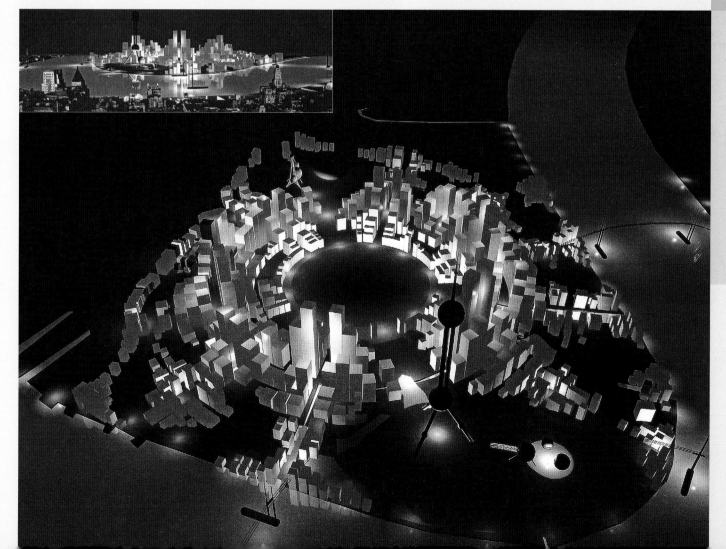

Global Perspectives:
Learning from the Other Side

From her vantage point in South Africa, Chrisna du Plessis of the Programme for Sustainable Human Settlement, CSIR Boutek, and guest-editor Brian Edwards challenge the accepted Western view that the key to sustainability lies in the advancement of new technologies. They expose the limitations of the West's notion of sustainable development, based on a value system of individual wealth, and expound ethical arguments that are rooted in the systemic world-view of traditional cultures in developing countries.

Opposite
ECD Architects, Slimbridge
Visitor Centre,
Gloucestershire, 2000.
Designed as a visitor's centre
for the Wildfowl and Wetland
Trust, this building is in a
protected area for birds – a
particularly sensitive setting.

Above
Nicholas Grimshaw &
Partners, Eden Project,
Cornwall, 2000. This series
of geodesic domes is a High
Tech version of the Victorian
glasshouse.

When one looks around the world it is clear that there are distinct regional approaches towards sustainable architecture, based on the dominance of certain cultural paradigms within each region. This issue of Δ is an attempt to bring these regional examples to wider attention – to counter the tendency to believe that Western High Tech holds the key to global sustainability. The real concern of sustainability is not so much with the internationalisation of architectural thought, as with the celebration of difference – the recognition that local solutions have global importance too. This is even more important when we realise that each of these regional solutions, while making a valid contribution, is only one part of the puzzle. To really jump to the next paradigm, we need to understand how the pieces can support and balance each other.

Most regional solutions fall somewhere on the continuum between a mechanistic, technological approach and an ecosystemic, spiritual approach. The challenge is to find an approach that combines and transcends both.

Sustainability through Technology

Sustainable development, as propagated by the UN, governments in the developed world and the World Business Council for Sustainable Development, is essentially a Western concept. It may be dressed up in the emperor's new clothes, but it remains the old notion of controlling the processes of nature to the maximum benefit of mankind through technological fixes. 'Green' architecture, as found in the 'developed' world, also fixates on the technological imperative. Even when architects such as Yeang, Foster and Rogers turn towards natural systems for inspiration, the approach is still a technological one, that is, how to build a building that works like a termite nest (imitating nature in order to control it).

Green architecture is earthed in a technological reality. Building science and functionality have been the two dominant strands of form generation for at least a century. Since function quickly becomes obsolete in a world of rapid change, space has become more elastic and less specific. Buildings are big volumes with increasingly imprecise uses. Bigness is itself an issue, not at the cultural level addressed by Koolhaas but at the technological one. At a fundamental level technology allows us to convert resources into useful artefacts (from cities to mobile phones). Technology implies a blend of science and design – a human dimension is imparted by the creative thinkers who imagine the designed future. The designers impart cultural value – their role is to fashion technology. The challenge is to make this process more ecologically conscious, to see buildings as a marriage not only of use and technology, but also of fashion and ecology. Fashion in the sense of giving legitimacy and expression to a style, and ecology in the sense of providing a fundamental natural order which architecture engages in.

It is not what buildings are but what they do and how they do it that is the major concern of sustainable development. True sustainability changes everything – the space plan, section and details of construction. If an ecological approach does not change social space and city form, it will have failed to become mainstream. However, sustainability also requires a change in the level of social values, and while Western-style science and technology can help us to mimic natural systems we have to turn elsewhere for appropriate social models.

Finding New Models of Living

As stated earlier, sustainable development as promoted internationally is a Western concept. Even the arguments used to sell sustainability are based on a Western value system founded on individual wealth and regarded as 'developed'. If we look at the UK Strategy for Sustainable Construction it is based on what is necessary to allow continued economic growth and further improve the bottom line. This view has resulted in arguments for sustainable development and construction which are founded on economic rather than ethical values. The resource-efficiency approach is driven by improved profits achieved through improved performance and cost savings. Sustainable construction is something investors and developers will only 'buy into' if there is a big enough market for it. Occupiers will only ask for sustainable buildings if they save money. Nowhere in this argument do ethics, and a sense of responsibility for the communal good, feature.

The interesting thing is that the international theoretical debates structuring the principles of sustainable development (Agenda 21, the Habitat Agenda, the Earth Charter), are propounding an ethical argument that has more in common with the world-view of the developing world than with that of the developed world.

This argument requires a systemic world-view that sees the planet and the world as one organism, a system that encapsulates countless subsystems which together form a part that is greater than the whole. Its very basis is a sense of the interconnectedness of everything in the dimensions of both space and time. It recognises

and reveres the seen and the unseen, the material and the immaterial, and the relationships that exist between the different elements that make up what we know as the 'world' (the ecosystem as well as human social systems). Survival of the entire system depends on the harmony that is achieved in and through these relationships.

Although this systemic world-view has largely been replaced by the mechanistic world-view as a result of successive waves of colonialism, it is espoused by most of the traditional cultures of the developing world. In these cultures, what the West terms 'sustainable development' is a way of life that is both practical and a deep spiritual and social obligation. Although this way of life is applied with various degrees of success it is still a lot closer to the ideals of sustainable development than the life style followed by most people in the developed world.

It is no surprise that the systemic world-view is dominant where people still live close to the earth. In these societies, men and women understand where the things they consume come from, and are acutely aware of the amount of energy required to transform raw materials into food, shelter and clothing. There is also a direct and visible correlation between the natural resources available and how much of these can be consumed. An intimate acquaintance with the cycles of nature further ensures that people are aware of how fragile survival is, and the extent to which it depends upon them having a harmonious relationship with their community and with nature. Therefore, two key concepts shape these societies: interconnectedness and impermanence.

Interconnectedness

The African concept of Ubuntu encapsulates the principle of interconnectedness and turns it into a system of ethics. Ubuntu is the understanding that a person is a person because of other people, and that how we conduct our relationships with others is of extreme importance. However, the term 'people' can be seen to include past and future generations, as well as the people of the animal, plant and spirit worlds. What we do, dream and think can have profound and unexpected repercussions on the entire network of life and energy. For instance, an unguarded thought or action can, several months later, result in the death by lightning of someone 50 kilometres away. For this reason, great care is taken to acknowledge the interconnectedness of everything and to maintain harmony between people, and also between the human world and the worlds of animals, plants, ancestors and nature spirits like the ones found in rocks and watercourses.

In the built environment interconnectedness is expressed in two ways. The first is by achieving physical

harmony with the cosmic order. In the Far East
the practice of feng shui strives to achieve
harmony and balance between the different
elements that make up the world and maintain
a beneficial flow of energy. Where one element
is dominant, energy cannot flow properly and
becomes stagnant. This results in disease,
discord in family relationships and money
problems (the flow of money is actually the flow
of energy). Feng shui concerns itself with the
placement and design of a building in
accordance with the natural environment and
the health and temperament of the inhabitants.
Care is also taken not to block the flow of the
earth's electromagnetic energy lines with
concrete structures, metal rods or other man-
made interferences. The principles found in
feng shui can also be found in the approach to
human health (acupuncture, t'ai chi, etc), thus
bringing the greater system of nature and the
systems of the human body into harmony.

The Western term 'sustainable development' is a way of life that is both practical and a deep spiritual and social obligation.

The Indian tradition of Sthapatya Ved is based
on the ancient Vedic philosophy that, just as
every cell in the body is connected to every other
cell, everything in the universe is connected
with everything else. Great care is taken to
harmonise buildings with nature and their
occupants through orientation, ventilation and
the use of locally available, natural materials.

This sense of interconnectedness is very
much a spiritual understanding of life which
leads to a reverence and respect for all of nature
that is expressed in the way buildings are placed
and resources used.

The other aspect of interconnectedness is
the paramount importance of the community
and the communal good, and the harmony achieved
within the community. In Africa, traditional kinship
obligations see the larger family group, and even
strangers, laying claim
to the proceeds of individual effort. How this affects
the built environment can be seen in the continent's
large cities. The World Bank estimates that in the 10
largest cities in Africa the average population density
is 193 people per hectare, with most people living in
informal settlements. Kinship obligations require
family members living in the city to extend shelter
and hospitality to any kinsman who comes there,
resulting in severe overcrowding and health problems.

In such a cultural context, wealth lies in social
relationships and not in property. Once the basic needs
of shelter have been taken care of, people will rather
invest in improving the education of the next generation
of children who, through kinship ties, will be obliged to
look after them in their old age. Alternatively, they will
invest money by providing loans or financial assistance
to other members of the community, thus expanding
their wealth base of social obligations and favours.

The strong focus on communal life also impacts
on the shape of urban space and on architecture.
The social structure of an extended family is expressed
in the layout of the homestead. Traditional African
homesteads consist of several separate rooms or huts
which are mainly used for sleeping and storage. The
general business of living takes place in the open
spaces between the buildings and these spaces are
planned as carefully as, if not with more care than,
the huts. The huts are grouped according to the social
standing of the inhabitants. Within a larger settlement,
the social standing of the head of a household is
expressed by where his homestead is positioned in
relationship to the homestead of the chief.

In India, houses are often built to accommodate
several families, with communal washing and cooking
facilities placed around a central courtyard. Here again,
there are separate spaces for individual family units
but the business of living happens in the communal
space. This model has been adapted with great success
in several Delhi government housing projects.

Impermanence
In agricultural societies there is an unquestioning
acceptance of the cycles of nature. What lives must
die when it is time for it to do so, and there is little
point in fighting it. The notion of impermanence is
central to Buddhist, Hindu and Taoist philosophy, and
change in whatever form is accepted with equanimity.

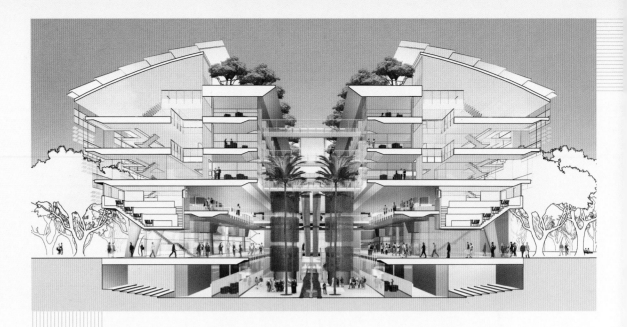

Above and opposite
Edward Cullinan Architects, Singapore Management University, Singapore, 2000. This is a verdant masterplan for a new campus in Singapore, in which the natural landscape is encouraged to sweep through, beneath and between the buildings. A notable feature is the way Cullinan's office has looked to vernacular architecture as a model. Devices similar to those found in traditional Singapore – shading trees, narrow sheltered streets and courts – are employed to create comfortable transitional spaces which minimise on the requirements for air conditioning. Energy-efficient building services, such as combined heat and power and absorption cooling, solar water heating and photovoltaic electricity generation, have also been proposed by the architects.

This acceptance of impermanence applies to the built environment as well. Conservationists have had great difficulty setting up programmes to conserve the architectural heritage of Eastern countries, as their traditions hold that even buildings should be allowed to die. It is the idea of the temple, and the place on which it is built, that is sacred and should be preserved. The temple building is just a vehicle for the sacred and therefore this 'body' should be allowed to die and the temple reincarnated into a new 'body' in accordance with the cycle of life and death.

In the mainly pastoral traditional societies of sub-Saharan Africa, buildings are not necessarily meant to outlast their owners, and no large public ones are transferred from generation to generation. Traditionally, buildings are built according to deep ecological standards of sustainability. Using renewable, biodegradable materials available on site, they leave only the footprints of their foundations when their time has come. Simple and confined to the bare necessities of shelter, these buildings also embody the idea of sufficiency. In contrast to Western norms, wealth and the desire for immortality are not expressed through the built environment.

Lessons for the West

The concepts of impermanence and inter connectedness bring certain principles to the debate about sustainable development and construction, principles from which the West can learn.

The first is sufficiency, mentioned above. This means building only what is necessary and not using more than is necessary. It is more than resource efficiency, which requires making the most efficient use of resources that will be used in any case. Sufficiency means architects are becoming conscious of the resource implications of every millimetre drawn on plan, and striving to reduce those millimetres to the bare minimum required. According to this principle, a 400-square-metre house for four people can have all the resource-efficient gadgets known to mankind, but it would still not be sustainable because its owners are using more resources than they need.

The second is the principle of responsible stewardship. The idea that land (actually all of nature) cannot be owned by an individual is common amongst the traditional cultures of developing countries, from India through Africa to the cultures of Native Americans. 'But how can you buy or sell the sky? The land? The idea is strange to us. If we do not own the freshness of the air and the sparkle of the water, how can you buy them?' Chief Seattle asked US president Franklin Pierce in 1854.

This explains why so many cultures 'traded' land with colonial forces – they simply did not understand the concept of landownership. In its place is the idea of responsible stewardship. An individual or group can make use of land, or a watercourse, as long as it is done in a responsible manner. Various social structures and laws regulate this. In southern Africa, security of tenure is achieved through right of use which is granted by the chief and his council of elders as the custodians of the land; but it is a right that is conditional on the responsible management of that land. In Burkina Faso in West Africa certain families or tribal groupings have the sacred duty to manage and take care of specific watercourses. In ancient Egypt, the gravest sin was to dam the waters of the Nile and thus take control of a resource that belonged to all.

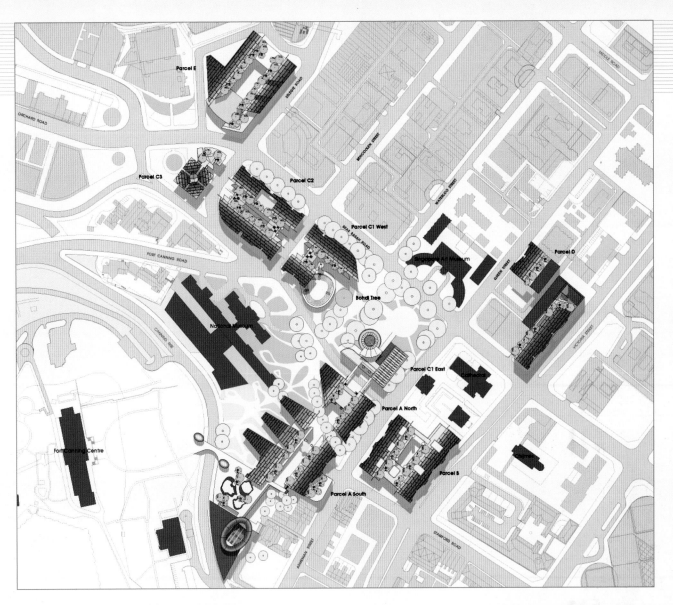

In the West, where buildings are seen as investments that should be transferable to future generations, and therefore durable, landownership is essential to provide security for that investment. However, if we look at the modern commercial property industry where buildings are designed for a 20-year life span, this system may not be the best option. Currently designers are battling to provide the flexibility that would allow for a longer life span. Instead, why not build fully dismountable buildings and give property developers a 20-year lease on a prime site, with renewal of the lease dependent on their responsible stewardship of the environment?

The third is the principle of social responsibility. In societies where the interest of the community, and not the individual, is paramount, decisions are taken to benefit the community. In architecture this means more than public consultation and participation. It means using resources to construct buildings that serve the needs of the community and not the short-term profit-taking of a developer. It means using the opportunity provided by the construction of a new building to empower members of the

community. This can be done by using local suppliers and labour, but also by providing on-the-job training. A good example of social responsibility in action is the initiative of MAS Architects in South Africa. Realising that their corporate clients were on the lookout for innovative and creative ideas for furniture, they trained welders who were making security gates to create High Tech furniture which their clients are now raving about – and then set them up to run their own company. The stonemason at Westcliffe Estate in Johannesburg was similarly empowered. The architects not only taught him to build in stone, they also taught him the basics of running his own business. By the end of the project a former pieceworker had the skills and contacts necessary to manage his own business and employ other people in the community.

The last, and probably most difficult, principle is to remember and acknowledge the spirituality inherent in, and encouraged by, the built environment. David Stea wrote: 'The West separates the mundane from the religious spatially and expects this to hold true everywhere. It is not always recognised that there is an element of the sacred in much mundane architecture.'[1] Probably the simplest example of this is the Indian woman who crawls out of her palm-leaf shelter each morning and draws a beautiful Rangoli pattern with coloured powder in the dust on her threshold, in a ritual

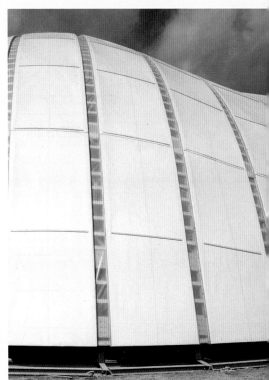

that connects her household to the patterns of life and the universe. In Africa, too, women redecorate their huts according to the phases of the moon, the seasons or to mark major life events, connecting the household intimately to the cycles of nature and human life. That is what spirituality in architecture means – connecting the user of a building to the rhythms of nature and the greater cosmos through the use of light and material, and the definition and use of space.

Oriental philosophy holds that man, the building he lives in and the city within which that building stands are all models of the cosmos and that disharmony at any of these levels causes disharmony at all levels. Global warming is showing us how intimately the decisions and actions of a person within the built environment, and the performance and properties of that built environment, can influence the global environment. And global warming is just one of many examples of how our decisions, and the values upon which they are based, can cause disharmony at a global level and eventually affect our individual survival. In terms of mankind's survival, it therefore becomes imperative that we bring our development activities into harmony with the workings of nature and the universe, and begin to accept responsibility for this. Harmony between mankind, the built environment and the universe can be created through reverence, acknowledging the interdependence of humans and nature on many levels, and respecting the community and its rituals.

Transcending the Grey Present for a Global Green Future

The Earth Charter states it quite clearly: 'The choice is ours: form a global partnership to care for Earth and one another or risk the destruction of ourselves and the diversity of life'.[2] To achieve this partnership, fundamental changes are needed in our values, institutions and ways of living. We have the technology to reduce our impact on the environment, but technology is not enough. We also need a value system that sees appropriate technologies implemented proactively as a matter of principle, and not as a reaction to a problem that suddenly threatens the bottom line of a company or because new legislation aimed at improving human health demands them.

At the same time, the value system must play watchdog over technology and the horrors it can unleash under the cover of solving a particular world problem. Nuclear scientists honestly

Spirituality in architecture means connecting the user of a building to the rhythms of nature and the greater cosmos through the use of light and material.

believe they are doing good by providing a 'clean' source of energy, biogeneticists are working towards alleviating world hunger and poverty. When looked at in isolation, both these technologies are wonderful. However, their impact on the system can have, and has already had, horrific consequences. In both cases there are other less dangerous and simpler answers. Answers that are rejected because they are not high tech enough, or complicated enough, to satisfy the West's fixation on technological growth and development. So building a house with earth blocks is not good enough. We have to first develop a machine that compresses the earth and add some (environmentally dubious) additives to the mixture in order to bring it up to our standards of technological development. If we are serious about sustainable construction, this is crazy. Not only is it unnecessary but it increases the costs of building for the millions who already cannot afford housing, while manufacturing and transporting the machines and additives places an unnecessary strain on the environment.

The next step towards more sustainable construction would be to temper this obsession with the technological fixes of the 'unsustainably developed' world with principles from the 'sustainably developing' world. Often, all that needs to change is the way we interact with our environment. Accept that all things must die, no matter how hard we try to fight this. Acknowledge your individual responsibility to take care of the community of life through your actions, as your wellbeing is interdependent with the wellbeing of the world. And finally, respect and revere the precious miracle of the web of life, and express it in your architecture for all to experience. ∆

Opposite
Shigeru Ban with Buro Happold, Japanese Pavilion, Hanover Expo, 2000. Constructed from a lattice structure of thin recycled cardboard tubes, the pavilion was covered with a roof of specially developed waterproof and fireproof paper. Even the foundations were recyclable. They were made of mass sand enclosed above ground with scaffolding boards supported by steel frames.

Notes
1. D Stea, 'The 10 Smudge Pots of Vernacular Building: Notes on Explorations into Architectural Mythology' in M Turan (ed), *Vernacular Architecture*, Avebury (Aldershot), 1990, pp 20–30.
2. See www.earthcharter.org

45

Bringing Together Head, Heart and Soul –
Sustainable Architecture in South Africa

Chrisna du Plessis describes how South African 'green' architecture is founded on the Ubuntu principles of interconnectedness and interdependence, in which man and nature, and nature and community, are understood to be integral. It is an approach which has helped to make social sustainability a characteristic of contemporary architecture, whether it is applied to High Tech commercial buildings or hands-in-the-mud community architecture.

The South African view of sustainable architecture encompasses far more than the mechanics of energy efficiency and improved performance and durability. Apart from a common-sense approach to resource efficiency, it has a strong desire to encourage social harmony, as well as an emotional connection to both the land and its cultures. Rooted in an ecosystemic world-view that is the heritage of a pastoral and agriculturalist life style, sustainable architecture in South Africa tries to express a heartfelt, almost spiritual response to the African context and the need to belong in and care for a beloved country. At the same time, it is driven by the pragmatism and rational, scientific approach of the mechanistic world-view. This results in an interesting spread of work ranging from the intellectual European style 'green' architecture that strives to improve the performance of conventional construction practices, to a reinterpretation of traditional architectural forms and values that aims to create a 'house for the soul'. The case studies discussed illustrate how the approaches differ from one end of the sustainability spectrum to the other, while all trying to create an architecture that is more than the 'green materialism' of ecologically approved buildings that are still hurtful to the spirit. An architecture that is true to the roots of South Africa.

The Historical Context – Living with the Land
South African 'green' architecture is founded on the principles of interconnectedness and interdependence. These principles form the basis of the African philosophy of Ubuntu. They are also found in the work of early Afrikaner thinkers and are encapsulated in the philosophy of holism promoted by General Jan Smuts, erstwhile prime minister of South Africa and one of the founding fathers of the modern United Nations.

Both the indigenous people and those European settlers who made South Africa their heartland followed an approach to the creation of buildings that is based on the understanding that man and nature, and individual and community, are interdependent. Their architecture was simultaneously a pragmatic response to the exigencies of a survivalist life style, and a deeply spiritual response to a sense of connection with the land, with nature and its cycles, and with the community. Historically, both the indigenous and the settler homesteads were characterised by climate-conscious design, the efficient use of local materials and the use of

agglomerations of small individual buildings and delineated outdoor spaces to house the various functions of a household. This allowed for flexibility and growth in the design. The building and its environment were not seen as separate entities, but as integrated, though different, aspects of a holistic life style.

In a sense, this early architecture of grass or mud huts and 'hartebeeshuisies' can be seen as the ultimate in green architecture. Made from local, renewable resources and using communal labour, the buildings were also completely biodegradable, leaving just stone foundations that could be reused or recycled. A conspicuous characteristic of these homesteads was their self-sufficiency and the fact that every resource was used to its fullest potential.

At the beginning of the 20th century two main formal architectural traditions could be found in South Africa. The one was a direct import from Europe, with scant attention paid to the context: the Neoclassicism of Herbert Baker and the corrugated-iron and cast-iron 'kit houses' imported to house the officials of the British Empire. The other was an attempt by Afrikaner architects to find a regional architecture that married the European traditions they were taught with the traditions, climate and materials of a continent with which they had built emotional links. While not consciously 'green', this architectural movement fulfils many of the requirements of green architecture, while attempting to find an aesthetic that is culturally and contextually appropriate.

Early architects such as Gerhard Moerdyk, and artists JH Pierneef and the Preller brothers, supported an organic and emotive response to the context which drew its inspiration from both indigenous and settler traditions. Their attempts at combining indigenous spatial layouts and decorative traditions with European construction methods and building forms continues to influence architects and inspired a host of 'African' game lodges. A different approach was followed by the next generation of architects. Inspired by the spirit that drove Frank Lloyd Wright, architects such as Norman Eaton, Karel Jooste and later Barrie Biermann adapted the clean lines and economy of Modernism to local materials, techniques, skills levels and climate, to develop what was to become known as Pretoria Regionalism.

Fisher describes Pretoria Regionalism as 'reflecting a particular response to nature and the landscape through the economical use of naturally available and industrially produced materials with an empirical response to climate.'[1] It is an architecture characterised by screens, verandas, pergolas and deep-set windows and eaves. The materials used were stock bricks, gum poles, stone and rough-cast exposed concrete, with thatched or corrugated-iron roofs. Set in lush indigenous gardens, these buildings were designed to be a part of nature, often blurring the boundaries between inside and outside.

The political climate of the 1980s and 1990s saw a greater emphasis being placed on addressing the social inequities engendered by apartheid, and restoring the social fabric of the country. The work of community architects like Ettienne Bruwer, Heinrich Kammeyer, Peter Rich and Carin Smuts primarily tried to achieve harmony within the community. The 'green' features they introduced were a pragmatic, common-sense solution to improving levels of comfort. Furthermore, the poverty of their clients prompted an architecture of sufficiency – not using more materials than is absolutely necessary and designing flexible, multipurpose spaces with robust detailing adapted to local skills levels. This was combined with the use of local labour, often trained during the construction process, and a design process that involved the community and resulted in appropriate solutions to their real needs.

The emotional response to the land and its people was replaced by a rational approach to the issues of resource efficiency, which uses passive solar design and high-tech solutions to reduce energy use and manage waste and water.

Come 1994 and South Africa's return to the international fold, this rich history of sustainable architecture was sidelined as politically incorrect (linked to the Afrikaner regime) and too technologically backward for a country that aims to be the African superpower. The emotional response to the land and its people was replaced by a rational approach to the issues of resource efficiency, which uses passive solar design and high-tech solutions to reduce energy use and manage waste and water, while continuing to

use conventional construction methods and materials such as steel and concrete. This approach was mainly imported by the multinational construction and design companies who were entering South Africa and is based on the green architecture movement of the industrialised world.

Despite practices such as Holm, Jordaan, Holm pioneering the rational approach as early as 1985 with the headquarters of the Building Industry Federation of South Africa, it was slow to take off. It is only in the past three years that pressure from international clients, and initiatives such as the Green Buildings for Africa programme driven by the CSIR, that we have begun to see results in the form of actual buildings. What adds a South African flavour to the approach is the incorporation of social sustainability into the construction process. As empowerment and job creation are two cornerstone requirements of government procurement policies, companies are forced to make social sustainability part of their business. This can take the form of joint ventures with previously disadvantaged companies, the training of local labourers in new skills that enable them to set up their own businesses, or the use of labour-intensive construction methods and locally manufactured materials.

This rational and pragmatic approach is followed not only by corporate clients but also by those working towards improvements in housing. As early as 1951, the National Building Research Institute was undertaking research on passive solar design in low-cost housing. This work was largely forgotten in the political turmoil of the 1970s and 1980s and only resurfaced when the Integrated Departmental Task Team on Environmentally Sound Low-cost Housing was formed to develop a set of guidelines for developers to follow. NGO-driven pilot projects such as Kutlwanong, a community-driven housing project near Kimberley, and the All Africa Games Village in Johannesburg illustrate the benefits of passive solar design principles, but the mainstream uptake has been minimal. This is mainly because the housing subsidy is not large enough to pay for simple energy-efficient features.

Another major obstacle towards more sustainable mass housing is the rejection of alternative technologies despite major cost savings to the home owner. For example, while community centres built of earth such as the Alliance Française Centre (Mitchell's Plain, Cape Town) are readily accepted, home owners are reluctant to accept earth construction as a viable alternative to the more conventional cement-block construction used in low-cost housing. There is also a low level of awareness of the benefits of energy- and water-efficiency measures and, as has happened in the All Africa Games Village, residents remove many of these features to install more conventional fixtures.

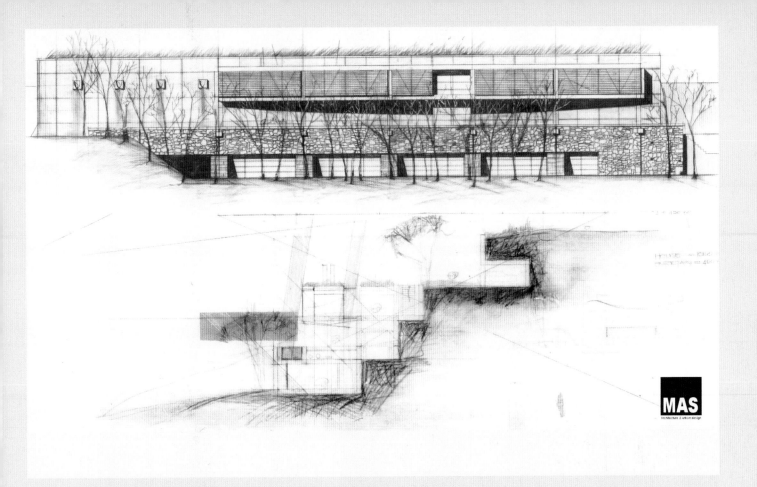

The Case Studies

Three small practices have been selected and their approaches range from the High Tech commercial to hands-in-the-mud community architecture. Together they epitomise the combination of head, heart and soul found in South African sustainable architecture.

An African House for the 21st Century – MAS Architects

MAS Architects is a small architectural and urban design practice that serves mainly corporate clients. The vision of the practice is to achieve synergy between technology and nature while providing desirable, healthy spaces. This is backed by a strong empowerment focus in their procurement and employee-development policies.

In 1998 the practice was approached by the owner of Westcliffe Estate in Johannesburg with the brief to design a 21st-century African house. The design team and the client concluded that the architecture of this century would be epitomised by the coming together of information technology and environmental responsibility in buildings designed for people within their local context. To achieve this synergy, the emphasis in the design of this family house was placed on resource management. The north orientation of the building, with large shading devices and dark wood shutters, reduces heating and cooling requirements. The stone wall that backs the house acts as a heat battery and also stimulates the convection currents that draw in cool air over the swimming pool, thus cooling the entire house. Natural gas meets all the heating requirements with excess heat used to warm the swimming pool. To manage energy use efficiently all lights, appliances, heating and security features are controlled from centrally located touch screens linked to a central computerised system. In addition to energy conservation, rainwater is captured in enormous tanks in the basement and is used to irrigate the garden and flush the toilets. Excess water is led through agricultural drains, lessening the need for an elaborate storm-water installation and replenishing the ground-water system.

Stone from the site is used for cladding and to fill the gabion baskets covering the front facade, and material reclaimed from other site excavations was used to build the retaining walls. Most of the wood in the house is reclaimed from decommissioned African mines. The interior was designed to be very flexible, with most of the partitioning reconfigurable. As the family owns an extensive art collection which is currently housed all over the world, the house was also designed to eventually become a venue for a permanent exhibition of the collection, thus extending its usable life span. The house is also constructed according to ISO 14000 principles of environmental management.

The trickier question was what would make the house African. As it is built for an extended family, it was seen as a village with the different functions accommodated in separate wings linked by communal spaces. In traditional villages, the tree and the river are the key places of social interaction, and therefore the central meeting space was envisioned as being under the village thorn tree, with the river flowing in front.

Above and previous spread
MAS Architects, Westcliffe Estate, 1998.

Situated on the steep slopes of one of old Johannesburg's hills, the site is visible from miles away, and the client did not want to contribute to the existing visual pollution. The house was therefore designed to eventually fade into the natural features of the hill. Its concrete structure is clad in stone from the site so that it resembles a continuation of the cliff face, with the 'tree room' itself reading as a cave in the mountainside. The central cantilevered roof is covered in oxidised copper and the other roofs are planted with indigenous vegetation. The entire site is rehabilitated and planted with indigenous vegetation to restore the degradation caused by the building process.

Westcliffe Estate is a good example of commercial 'green' architecture. It uses conventional concrete and steel construction, but introduces sustainability through the energy and water systems, recycled stone from the site, indigenous landscaping, natural ventilation and passive thermal design.

Excavating Forgotten Knowledge – Archeo-Architects

Director Francois Lötter of Archeo-Architects describes the practice's work as an attempt at excavating the lost common-sense knowledge of both physical and spiritually sustainable living, while developing a regional aesthetic that is based on the traditional shapes and materials of indigenous architecture.

House Mosedi in Johannesburg was built for a client who wanted a 'spiritual' house that would connect him to his African roots while living lightly on the land. The process of designing and building was unexpectedly emotional and turned into a spiritual journey for both architect and client, during which they had to rethink many of their preconceptions about both interpersonal relationships and the relationship between man and nature and man and the cosmos. Many of the ecologically friendly systems that were designed for the house were rejected by the city council and, in the end, the 'green' part of the building was limited to the materials used. Thatch, gum poles and rock from the site were used together with construction materials rescued from demolition sites.

The ideas developed during the design of House Mosedi were taken further in the next project. The owner's house of the Thaba Ya Batswana guesthouse complex in the Magalies mountains west of Johannesburg is an emotive response to the Shona ruins found on site and the grand vistas of the landscape. Built on a stone plinth, the primary form-giver of the homestead is a combination of circular and rectangular shapes used by the Shona people. Windows are deep-set or covered by large roof overhangs. The entire house is run on solar power, with a backup generator for the few days a year when the sun is not enough. Grey water and black water are separated, filtered and recycled on site, while large rainwater storage tanks are built out of local stone. No formal garden will be planted and the indigenous vegetation disturbed by construction is rehabilitated.

Together the two houses illustrate the difficult juggling act of reconciling conventional construction

Above
Archeo-Architects, House Mosedi, Johannesburg, Magalies, 2000.

practice, as accepted by councils, contractors and clients, with a more environmentally friendly and romantic approach to architecture.

Building with Soul – Greenhaus Architects

Over the years Ettienne Bruwer has acquired a reputation as an architect who builds with soul. He describes his work as an attempt to reconcile the formative principles of metamorphosis and sacred geometries with the 'green' agenda in a buoyant, dynamic way. Working with natural materials such as cob and strawbale, and following an aesthetic directed by anthroposophical principles, his buildings are organic yet practical, sensuous yet functional.

Working in community architecture, Ettienne's playful workshops encourage communities to work together. In that way, the process of building also helps to restore balance and harmony within them. A good example of his community-orientated, hands-on yet spiritual, approach is the Uluntu Centre in Guguletu, Cape Town. In 1990 the Urban Foundation approached the architects (Bruwer and Johnson) because they were anxious to combat the vandalism and resentment that the community was targeting at the 'industrial sheds' that had previously been built. Meetings with local people went on for nine months before the community decided what their space requirement priorities were. The designs were then developed with the adults through clay workshops. This resulted in a building that consists of 'indoor' spaces set in a matrix of conversational 'outdoor' spaces formed by the undercover circulation spaces. Low budgets called for innovation – carved wooden salad bowls became light fittings and the architect himself stained the glass.

This idea of the building as a narrative of indoor and outdoor spaces, enabling conversations between humans and nature, continues in the practice's residential architecture. A house in Johannesburg is described as negotiating archetypal experiences – 'in a boat', 'along the cliff', 'down the hill', 'the spirit that is behind the wall.' There are neither courtyards nor passages, only openings that breathe into opened inside spaces where man and the elements, fauna and flora, can mingle 'intimately and rhythmically'.

The 'green' features are woven without thought into the spiritual being of all Bruwer's buildings. They are not add-ons but an intrinsic feature of the poetry in the architecture; spontaneous inventions that run as a theme through the building.

In Conclusion

In the past 50 years political agendas and economic policies have done much to destroy the traditions of interconnectedness and interdependence with nature found in South African architecture. Elements of it remain, however, in the work of a few inspired idealists, whether they approach it from the head, the heart or the soul. What is required now is a new design paradigm, where environmentally friendly features are included not because of profit motives or regulations, but because they form an intrinsic part of the building's essential harmony. Δ

The View from Australia

Green Limits in a Land of Plenty

As Australia enters the 21st century it leaves behind it the cultural uncertainty of the 'white fellas' and finds a new multicultural confidence, which should be smoothing the way for a green agenda. Lindsay Johnston from the University of Newcastle, New South Wales, gives an overview of sustainability in Australian architecture and describes two 'mid green' projects and one 'deep green' project.

'White man got no dreaming, him go 'nother way, White man, him go different. Him got road belong himself'. *Aboriginal elder.*

Australia is a paradox. On the one hand a fledgling culture barely 200 years old and on the other the oldest extant culture on Earth, 50,000 years old. Physically, the sixth largest country on Earth with a landmass of three million square miles (7.6 million square kilometres) – just smaller than the USA. A climate that ranges from arid desert through tropical rainforest and temperate lowlands to alpine mountain. A population of merely 19 million crowded around the edges,[1] and yet one of the highest per capita carbon-emitters in the world.

'White fellas' in Australia have agonised over identity since their arrival, many as convicts. The 'cultural cringe' and 'hanging on to mother's apron strings' have engaged commentators on the Australian condition. This uncertainty is reflected architecturally in texts such as Robin Boyd's The Australian Ugliness, where imported Classicism gives way to imported Modernism with the worst characteristics of Europe or America.[2]

Today doubt has given way to self-assurance. 'Sydney 2000' and the 'Freeman Factor' have finally brought white Australians to understand who they are. Only a recalcitrant Howard government precludes a republic, an apology to the indigenous peoples for wrongs of the past and a serious attempt to take a responsible position on the environment. Colonial Australia has metamorphosised into multicultural Australia.

In the psyche, the genius of Australia lies in the arid centre, in the eucalyptus forests and on the beautiful beaches.[3] The fierce strength of the red ochre deserts and Uluru, the dappled delicacy of the leafs of gregarious trees, roots knotted in rock faces, and the shimmering blue of the water. So different to Europe, Asia and North America.

The fundamental way of building is different, the materials are different and the climate is different. Early building paradigms came to the southeast of the continent and this essay follows conditions and examples from that part. Whereas buildings in northwest Europe were made from stone with mass and inherent structural stability, early Australian buildings were lightweight timber-framed buildings that required inherent techniques of bracing. The arrival of corrugated iron in the mid-19th century as ballast in ships from Britain brought a seminal introduction to the architecture of the country.[4] The later importation of iron-framed 'kit' homes and churches from the foundaries of Scotland developed a tradition that has led to the lightweight steel-framed architectural technologies of today.[5]

Cultural baggage has delayed the understanding of sustainable building within the climatic context of Australia. Misappropriated Classicism gave way to misappropriated Modernism. In housing particularly, what Boyd called 'Featurism' has given us 'Fediterranean' (nostalgic neo-Federation and Mediterranean) and 'ABBA' (all bloody balustrades and arches). The dreaded 'brick venereal disease' permeates the suburban sprawl, with most Australian homes inappropriately built of timber frame with a brown brick veneer and dark tiled roof – no roof ventilation and walls with thermal mass on the outside – the opposite of what is required. Many of Australia's non-residential buildings are glass boxes pumped full of fossil-fuel energy to sustain them. Today, misappropriated international architectural 'isms' continue, inspired from the ethersphere through the crown of the skull, with disregard for place or climate, rather than from the loci through the soles of the feet.

The lineage of a contemporary Australian architecture that is responsive to place and climate emerged through the earlier works of Harry Seidler as an Australian Gropius or Le Corbusier, through Syd Ancher as an Australian Aalto and, particularly, through Glenn Murcutt as an Australian Mies.[6] Seidler's later works are significant examples of climate-responsive buildings with sun shading and innovative energy-efficient systems. Murcutt should take credit for making respectable the Australian 'vernacular' of corrugated iron and for authoring a portfolio of built work, and an associated polemic,[7] on the Australian landscape, climate, topography, hydrology, geology, flora and fauna – 'touch this earth lightly.'[8] There are others, too many to mention, who have developed a climate-responsive Australian architectural language that responds to culture and place.[9]

Also, the writing and associated graphic illustrations of Australian environmentalist Bill Mollison, who expounded the concept of 'permaculture',[10] have

permeated the work of many Australian architects and inspired architects and environmentalists internationally. The key to his proposed solutions to the problems of self-sufficiency and sustainability is integration of thinking – an understanding of the interconnectedness of natural and man-generated systems.

The 'green agenda' has been supported for many years by individuals and groups within the Royal Australian Institute of Architects, although the corporate position might still be seen as less committed. The RAIA Environment Design Guides, now under the umbrella of the Council of Building Design Professions, are a primary reference. The Australian Building Energy Council is an industry body with a mission to liaise with government and to establish voluntary best practice criteria in building energy performance. There is now progress towards mandatory minimum standards for energy use in housing through NatHERS (the National Housing Energy Rating Scheme), and in all buildings through the Building Code of Australia. The NSW Sustainable Energy Development Authority has a star-rating scheme for office buildings, based on greenhouse gas emissions, and has established a 'green power' option for supplying electricity sourced from renewable energy sources from the grid. The government is systematically auditing energy use in its own buildings. The government Australian Greenhouse Office is charged with addressing the national reduction of greenhouse gas emissions. Any systematic assessment of embodied energy in buildings appears a long way off.

Towards a 'Green' Classification

Looking beyond basic sun control, there is an emerging 'taxonomy of green'. Low-technology solutions for simple, environmentally sustainable life styles are described as 'light green' – the villager in the developing world, the frugal retreat in the bush. High-technology solutions that progress towards sophisticated, comfortable, partially environmentally sustainable life styles are described as 'mid green' – much of today's 'green' architecture, the high-embodied-energy building covered in sun shading devices or photovoltaic panels. Holistic low-energy or resource-efficient solutions that can deliver a sophisticated, comfortable and environmentally sustainable life style are described as 'deep green' – there are very few examples so far in Australia.

Two Mid-Green Case Studies
Peter Stutchbury and EJE Architecture in association with the Faculty of Nursing, University of Newcastle, NSW.

The Faculty of Nursing at the University of Newcastle is one facet of the university's agenda to procure good quality 'green' buildings and transform an established 130-hectare campus into a naturally functioning ecosystem. The campus is located 160 kilometres north of Sydney, 10 kilometres from the sea to the west of the city of Newcastle and is in natural bushland with extensive eucalyptus trees and wetlands. Inspired by the writings of Bill Mollison, mowed lawns have been replaced by swales and native vegetation to control water flow, reduce erosion, rescue natural wetlands and renew natural wildlife. The Newcastle climate is similar to Sydney's with summer temperatures reaching 38°C with high humidity and winter temperatures falling to about 4°C.

Designed by Peter Stutchbury[11] in association with EJE Architecture, following a limited competition, the project develops from the work and teaching of Richard Leplastrier[12] from the precedents of Glenn Murcutt and from the earlier Design Building on the campus by the same architects. It is a fine demonstration in a larger building of the distinctive Australian 'corrugated iron' architectural vocabulary. Sophisticated computer simulations of ventilation, thermal performance and

lighting was carried out by Advanced Environmental Concepts including CFD modelling (computational fluid dynamics).

The building forms an extension to an existing building that did not respond well to climatic circumstances. Orientation of the new building is thus not ideal, with long facades facing east and west. The building consists of two 3–4-storey wings of academic offices and a central auditorium. Only the auditorium is air-conditioned. A major feature of the project is a geothermal field that exploits the stable ground temperature of 17°C to provide a source of heat in winter and to dissipate heat in summer.

The offices are in single loaded wings, six metres wide, to facilitate natural cross ventilation and natural light penetration. The structure is concrete with high thermal mass and precast floor slabs with some potential for disassembly. External walls locate the thermal mass on the inside with insulation on the outside and cladding in corrugated sheet steel. Interiors have exposed concrete floors and frugal finishes with minimal decoration. Internal walls are faced in recycled Australian hardwood planks. Light transfer-glass floor panels allow light penetration into lower floor corridors. A steel-framed and corrugated-steel 'fly' or parasol roof over the office wings allows air movement and neutralises the heat of the sun. The facades are fitted with extensive sun-control devices, and light shelves to reflect natural light into the building.

Only the 450-seat auditorium has air conditioning and this uses displacement stack effect or buoyancy-driven air movement which delivers chilled air from a plenum under the seats. This system allows air contact with the concrete floor and faciliates night purging and subsequent recovery of 'coolth' from the thermal mass. Fresh air input is controlled by a gas sensor. The system can operate as a ventilation system only in moderate climatic periods. The air-conditioning system was the first in Australia to use a geothermal field to harvest heat from, and dissipate heat to, the ground through a water-filled circuit in 55 vertical boreholes 100 metres deep on a 4.5-metre grid.

A post-occupancy life-cycle analysis of this building evaluated embodied energy and utilisation energy. An associated study assessed the embodied energy in the additional materials in the parasol roof and the facades' sun-control devices. It was established that the additional embodied energy attributable to these features was recovered through utilisation-energy savings in four to six years, with associated long-term cost benefits. The project, which costs A\$7 million, shows the important role universities play in developing new sustainable technologies.

Bligh Voller Nield in association with Lobb Partnership, Stadium Australia, Sydney.
Stadium Australia was the main venue for the Sydney Olympics and the theatre for the opening and closing ceremonies and many of the sporting events, including

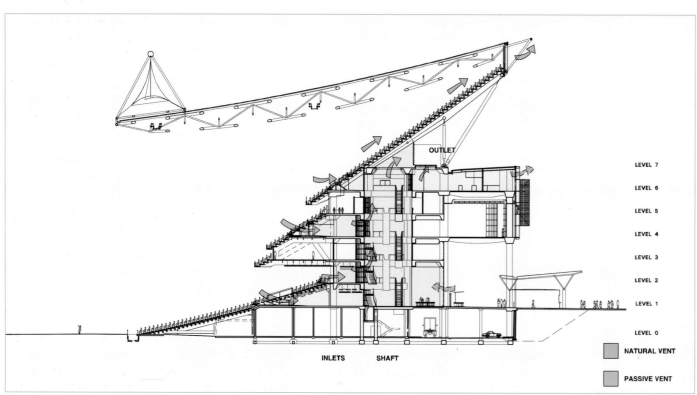

OUTLET	
	LEVEL 7
	LEVEL 6
	LEVEL 5
	LEVEL 4
	LEVEL 3
	LEVEL 2
	LEVEL 1
	LEVEL 0

INLETS   SHAFT

NATURAL VENT

PASSIVE VENT

aboriginal Australian Cathy Freeman's win in the womens' 400 metres – perhaps a defining moment in Australia's history.[13] Designed by architects Bligh Voller Nield, in association with Lobb Partnership of London, Stadium Australia is a 110,000-seat privately funded stadium on a degraded site, formerly the city abattoir, located near the demographic centre of Sydney and linked to an efficient public transport system which was one of the great success stories of the Olympic fortnight. Sydney temperatures in summer rise to 38°C with high humidity and winter temperatures fall to near zero.

A crucial strategy for longevity and adaptability required that after the games the stadium would be multi-use and would be reduced in size to an 80,000-seat venue suitable for rugby union and Australian rules football. The Olympic running track is to be removed and the low tier seating moved inwards. The high sections of the open end stands are to be removed and a roof introduced over the lower sections.

Energy use in the stadium is claimed to be 68 per cent of that of a 'conventional' stadium through use of sun shading, buoyancy-driven stack-effect natural ventilation, structural night cooling, efficient natural and artificial lighting and on-site gas co-generation.

A complex design process utilised life-cycle analysis to inform strategic and tactical design decisions in connection with determination of form and structure, materials selection, thermal and energy modelling, and cost-in-use evaluation. In the initial stages much attention was paid to reducing the bulk and mass of the building and optimising sight lines thus significantly reducing the height of the 900-metre-diameter structure, with associated savings in embodied energy and cost.

Energy use in the stadium is claimed to be 68 per cent of that of a benchmarked 'conventional' stadium through use of sun shading, buoyancy-driven stack-effect natural ventilation, structural night cooling, efficient natural and artificial lighting and on-site gas co-generation. Buoyancy-driven ventilation is induced through five large stacks built into each grandstand with computer-controlled dampers at inlets and outlets. Mechanical ventilation is provided for basement spaces, and air conditioning for the banqueting hall and some other spaces. Mechanical systems use night purging to cool the substantial thermal mass that emits 'coolth'

by day. Modelling was carried out by Short Ford Associates, the ECADAP Center, De Montford University, Cambridge Architectural Research and Max Fordham and Partners.

Rainwater is collected from the roofs and is stored in large basement tanks for pitch irrigation. The stadium is linked to a grey-water main which collects and treats grey water and returns it for use for toilet flushing and nonpotable purposes. Materials were evaluated for their environmental cost, health issues and long-term appropriateness. A genuine effort was made to address embodied-energy issues and to source lower energy options for materials. Timber used in the project was from sustainable sources with some recycled. Materials that use or emit toxins were excluded. PVC and CFC refrigerants were generally avoided. Two 500-kilovolt gas-fired co-generators are built into the project to produce electricity and hot water, and thus reduce demand for energy from the grid. Energy purchased from the grid adopts the 'green power' option, buying power sourced from wind turbines and solar farms. These various measures allowed the stadium to meet the green credentials of the Sydney Olympics.

Deep Green
Marci Webster-Mannison, Director of Design, Charles Sturt University, Thurgoona Campus, Albury, NSW
Albury is a country town on the Murray River, southeast of Sydney and 300 kilometres from the east and south coasts. Summer temperatures rise to 42°C, but with low humidity and cool clear nights, and winter temperatures falling to below freezing these are difficult conditions for low-energy buildings.

The Thurgoona Campus of Charles Sturt University is substantially a green-field site in undulating grassland with occasional trees. The design involved development of a masterplan and infrastructure. New buildings already completed include a School of Environmental and Information Sciences, a teaching complex that includes a 200-seat lecture theatre, a student union building and student residences. The masterplan and all the new buildings have been designed by the university director of design, Marci Webster-Mannison, in collaboration with Advanced Environmental Concepts, who carried out computer simulations, and a local specialist firm, Branco Boilers and Engineering, who assisted in the development of many of the ingenious services systems. The campus and buildings are an exemplar of holistic and integrated design thinking, following the principles of Bill Mollison's 'permaculture'. There is no mechanical air conditioning, there is no connection to the water main or sewer and composting toilets are used throughout.[14]

Site planning is derived from detailed site analysis of topography, vegetation and natural drainage patterns.

The pedestrian spine, roads and services follow contours punctuated by existing trees. Core, academic and residential precincts are defined by drainage paths.

The new buildings have 300 to 600 millimetre rammed-earth external and internal walls with roof structures made from recycled timber supplemented with some plantation timber. Roofs and sun screens are corrugated steel. Upper floors and ceiling slabs are in situ concrete to provide additional thermal mass. The main lecture theatre has an earth-covered concrete barrel-vault roof. Roofs have natural wool insulation. Walls are uninsulated. Material selection has been rigorous, with natural organic materials such as wool and linoleum, no use of PVC or MDF and specially prepared nontoxic paints. Low embodied-energy strategies have been carefully pursued and a wonderful shelving and glass flooring system used through all the buildings has been retrieved and recycled from a library in Sydney.

Buildings are sited on an east–west axis to maximise controllable solar access. Sun-shading devices and roof overhangs eliminate high summer sun and admit low winter sun. Clerestory windows and high windows in thermal stacks admit light into the centre of the buildings. Light wells and cast-glass floor panels allow natural light to penetrate to lower floors.

The high thermal mass is used effectively to moderate external temperatures, emitting warmth in winter and 'coolth' in summer. Solar access in winter warms the thermal mass and this is supplemented by a vast array of water-filled solar panels on the roof, at the critical angle for Albury of 37° pitch, which heat water stored in a large insulated tank. The water is circulated through polyethylene pipes cast in the concrete floor and ceiling slabs. In summer, the system is ingeniously used in reverse and the solar panels dissipate heat into the clear night sky thus chilling down the thermal mass to provide 'coolth' by day.

Natural stack-effect ventilation is induced by thermal chimneys, which are a feature of the roofscape, and air movement is adjusted by intake and outlet louvres controlled by computer. Natural ventilation to the earth-covered lecture theatre enters through a thermal labyrinth surrounded by thermal mass with mist-spray passive evaporative cooling as well as a geothermal-field heat exchange.

Storm water is collected by the waterways and passes through wetlands to sedimentation ponds at the bottom of the site, from where it is pumped by windmill to the top of the site for constant reticulation. This keeps it clear and, among other benefits, allows frogs – which minimise mosquitoes – to breed. Prominent steel water tanks integrated into the structures store collected rainwater. Grey water is cleansed using artificial wetlands and is disposed of as subsurface irrigation. All toilets are dry composting units on ground and upper levels, a unique feature for a public university campus.

Notes
1. Philip Drew, *The Coast Dwellers: Australians Living on the Edge,* Penguin Books (Ringwood, Vic), 1994.
2. Robin Boyd, *The Australian Ugliness,* Penguin Books (Ringwood, Vic), 1968.
3. Daryl Jackson, 'From Edge to Centre: Sense and Stylism', *UIA International Architect,* 4, 1984.
4. Anne Warr, 'The Technology of the Corrugated Shed' in Peter Freeman and Judy Vulker (eds), *The Australian Dwelling,* The Royal Australian Institute of Architects (Canberra), 1991, pp 85–91.
5. Alan Ogg, *Architecture in Steel: The Australian Context,* The Royal Australian Institute of Architects (Canberra), 1987.
6. Jennifer Taylor, *Australian Architecture Since 1960,* The Royal Australian Institute of Architects (Canberra), 1990.
7. Glenn Murcutt, 'Appropriateness in the Modern Australian Dwelling' in Freeman and Vulker *op cit,* pp 47–54.
8. Philip Drew, *Leaves of Iron,* The Law Book Company (Sydney), 1985, p 54.
9. Davina Jackson and Chris Johnson, *Australian Architecture Now,* Thames and Hudson (London), 2000.
10. Bill Mollison, *Permaculture: A Practical Guide to a Sustainable Future,* Island Press (Washington, DC), 1990.
11. Philip Drew, *Peter Stutchbury,* Pesaro Architectural Monographs Sydney, 2000.
12. Richard Leplastrier, 'Architecture and Place – Manifesto', *Architecture Australia,* vol 88, no1 (Jan/Feb 1999), pp 56–69.
13. Patrick Bingham-Hall, *Olympic Architecture: Building Sydney 2000,* Watermark Press (Sydney), 2000.
14. Lindsay Johnston, 'Deep Green – Charles Sturt Thurgoona Campus', *Architecture Review Australia,* no 73 (Spring 2000), pp 94–9.
15. George Wilkenfeld, 'Reducing Greenhouse Gas Emissions through Design of the Built Environment', RAIA/BDP Environment Design Guide, GEN 33, 2000.
16. Gareth Cole, 'Residential Passive Solar Design', Melbourne, RAIA/BDP Environment Design Guide, GEN 12, 1997.
17. Bill Mollison, op cit, p31.

Summary

In 200 years the 'white fella' has done possibly irreparable damage to a natural environment that has sustained human habitation for 50,000 years. The paradox is that rough tough Australia is in fact incredibly delicate. Problems include increased deforestation and salination from inappropriate crops, destruction of the land as a result of the introduction of inappropriate small hoofed animals, destruction of the waterways from erosion and pollution, and mining in culturally and environmentally sensitive areas. Today's buildings, cities, life style and resultant ecological footprint are sustained by cheap energy from nonrenewable sources, the price of which does not reflect its real cost – drawing down Earth's natural capital.

Australia's 2010 Kyoto Protocol commitments were negotiated as an increase in greenhouse gas emissions to 108 per cent of its 1990 emissions, when most other developed nations were targeting reductions. Australia's 1998 emissions were already at 117 per cent of 1990's and the country appears unlikely to meet its Kyoto commitments. Emissions from energy use in commercial buildings are projected to nearly double between 1990 and 2010, and overall building operating energy emissions are projected to rise 150 per cent over this period.[15]

Politically, the climate lacks 'bite'. The cult of privatisation has led to a lack of investment in green infrastructure, green energy production and innovative buildings. Free market competition and threats to deregulate the practice of architecture see a situation where 'cheapest is best', with little resultant investment in thorough and ground-breaking design or exemplary building solutions.

While there is a huge engagement with the 'green agenda' at both intellectual and practical levels, especially among individual architects and smaller practices, there is a dearth of exemplary examples of large 'green' buildings. An even greater challenge for Australia, beyond 'green' buildings, is 'green' cities. Australia's dispersed urban morphology is, like its housing design, largely inappropriate to the climate and based on high use of private cars. There are, however, emerging institutional initiatives and a growing sensibility to these issues.

Across the vast climatic variation, northern hemisphere solutions are seldom appropriate and yet often employed. How to keep cool is the main issue, rather than how to keep warm. Temperate areas of the continent have a relatively benign climate, with warm days and cool nights that are ideally suited to natural solar architecture that makes effective use of critical thermal mass for retention of warmth and 'coolth'. In the coastal areas, high humidity creates discomfort and demands air movement. In the hot humid tropics, thermal mass is of little value and air movement is crucial. Always, shade is important.

Strategies for energy-efficient housing design are well documented and yet not adequately applied – orientation, sun control, insulation, ventilation and thermal mass.[16] In commercial buildings, strategies such as double glazing and high-performance glass keep heat in as well as out, and do not eliminate the build-up of heat from machines and humans. Hybrid or naturally ventilated solutions are few and there appear to be no built examples in Australia of double ventilated facades. Few built examples of 'green' architecture go beyond the building footprint to consider wider issues of site, water, effluent, waste and transport. There remain many paradoxes in architectural practice and education with regard to the relationship between the international mainstream of media driven 'style' architecture and the crucial realities of ecological sustainability. △⊃

'The seemingly wild and naturally functioning garden of a New Guinean villager is beautifully ordered and in harmony, while the clipped lawns and pruned roses of the pseudo-aristocrat are nature in wild disarray.'[17]
—*Bill Mollison*

Ken Yeang

Green Questionnaire

What is your, or your practice's, definition of sustainable design?
Sustainable design can be defined as ecological design – design that integrates seamlessly with the ecological systems in the biosphere over the entire life cycle of the built system. The building's materials and energy are integrated, with minimal impact on the environment from source to sink.

What are your key concerns as a designer interested in sustainability?
My key concerns are that designers should be aware of the connectivity of all systems in nature and that these should be integrated as part of the built system's processes. Designers should also beware of making excessive claims about the sustainability of their designs because ecological design is still in its infancy.

How would you judge the success of a building in the 'green' age?
A successful 'green' building is one that integrates seamlessly with the natural systems in the biosphere, with minimal destructive impact on these systems and maximum positive impact.

In what way do you use nature as a guide?
Nature should be imitated and our built systems should be mimetic ecosystems. Δ

Above
Ken Yeang

This page, left
Waterfront House, Jalan Pinang (adjacent to the Petronas Twin Towers), Kuala Lumpur, design 2000.

This page, right
Tokyo-Nara Tower (urban site between Tokyo and Nara), design 2001.

Opposite page, left
EDITT Tower, Singapore, competition design 1998.

Opposite page, right
Elephant and Castle Eco-Towers, London, design 2000.

Sustaining Interactions Between the Natural and Built Environment in Singapore

Sustainable design has had minimal impact in Singapore where clients, developers and planning regulations tend to favour an 'international architecture', which bears little or no relation to the local climate and conditions. In spite of this, the Department of Architecture at the National University of Singapore is intent upon developing a 'New Asian Tropical Architecture' which reflects the strength of the indigenous culture and interacts closely with vegetation. Clive Briffet, associate professor in the department, describes what this will mean and three projects that are designed in response to their total environment.

'The central determinants that shape all human activities on the land are the elements of the self perpetrating biosphere that sustain life on earth.'[1]

Sustainable design in buildings has been discussed for some years in Singapore but attempts to implement sustainable architecture in practice have been minimal. Commentators on local architecture have advocated a need to introduce a vision of local architecture that has a tropical, or more precisely an equatorial, flavour which is more representative of native Asian cultural roots and more in harmony with nature. The attempts to produce sustainable architecture that utilises sustainable building construction techniques in a local context is therefore closely intertwined with the pursuit of the so-called tropical architecture concept. It is thus considered desirable to encourage local designs that more adequately reflect the strength of the indigenous culture and interact more closely with the native vegetation. However, this does not necessarily amount to a reversion to the traditional vernacular. The need to meet modern demands and to create new initiatives is still considered desirable and realistic.

The development of the 'New Asian Tropical Architecture' is the current mission of the Department of Architecture in the National University of Singapore. Numerous teaching initiatives, research and consultancy projects, seminars, conferences and competitions have been organised in recent years to achieve this. In practice, however, the opportunities to realise such an aim have so far been limited. This is because the planning and design of real estate development in Singapore is dictated firstly by a fairly rigid planning and building control system, secondly by a strongly financially orientated developer and owner fraternity, and, thirdly, by clients who prefer to recreate the standard package of worldwide city architecture. It seems that fame and status both for companies and architects in Singapore derive more from replicating designs of internationally famous buildings elsewhere than from developing an indigenous green architecture. In any city there are difficulties in producing architecture that has sufficient strength of character and affinity to be a representation of local culture and natural attributes. The economic perspective is clearly a dominating driving force but another, equally important, influence that should prevail is the way we think about building design.

The examples selected in this chapter are deliberately chosen to demonstrate that what is important in creating sustainable architecture is not just the building design itself but the total environment within which it is created, especially around and about the built complex. As noted by Ken Yeang, an ecologically friendly Malaysian architect:

> ... if we need to apply the ecosystem concept to design, then the project site must at the outset be conceived holistically by the designer as a unit consisting of both biotic and abiotic (living and nonliving) components functioning together as a whole to form an ecosystem, and before any human action can be inflicted on the project site, its features and interactions must be identified and fully understood.[2]

Ian McHarg in his seminal work on design with nature also noted that, 'each project site needs to be individually evaluated with consideration given to the ecosystem's own natural values, its processes, its constraints, and its inherent array of natural opportunities, all of which differ with different locations'.[3] In terms of architectural design Yeang further suggests that:

> ... the building may therefore be regarded as a form of energy and material resources that is managed and assembled by the designer into

a temporary form and then demolished at the end of the period of use, with the materials either recycled within the built environment or assimilated into the natural environment.[4]

The need to consider the built environment as being part of, and in harmony with, the natural environment is further reinforced by Geoffrey Bawa in Sri Lanka. Milroy Pereira, the practice's project architect, suggests that, 'the building should not always be designed to be looked at. It could also be considered as a structure to look from'.[5] And in his book on Bawa, Brace Taylor comments: 'Rarely do his designs allow the architecture to pre-empt the primordial importance of the natural surroundings.'[6]

Robert Powell, a locally based architect in Singapore who has published many texts featuring local buildings that incorporate tropical designs, comments that, 'the spirit of the tropical house is to merge the dwelling with its surroundings by creating ambiguous and intermediary spaces'.[7] Jimmy Lim, a Malaysian architect of environmentally friendly buildings, also confirms that, 'the climatic phenomena of heavy rain, strong sun and gentle trade winds should all be fully catered for in the design of such buildings'.[8]

The provision of wide overhanging roofs, shady tree surroundings and open, cross ventilated communal areas are therefore desirable features to attain. Tay Kheng Soon, who has been advocating the use of tropical architecture for many years in Singapore, believes that, 'a total environmental design approach should include nature conservation and ecological principles amongst its attributes'.[9] In relating how such principles can be incorporated even into high-rise design, Yeang in his discourse on the bioclimatic skyscraper justifies this approach as 'a comfort based rationale and a passive low energy one'.[10]

Case Studies

The case studies presented below all draw on these principles and confirm that, 'ecological processes should become the central determinant of form for all human activities'.[11]

Bukit Timah Nature Reserve Interpretation Centre

This simple timber-framed low-rise building was mainly constructed of local Malaysian timber and has timber shingles on steeply sloped pitched roofs. The architectural vocabulary has been described as a 'vernacular tropical design appropriate with the natural setting'.[12] The centre, designed by Thomas Wong Kok Woh, provides a convenient arrival point as it is strategically located at the entrance to the last remaining area of primary forest found in Singapore. This forest is home to over 600 species of trees, 100 species of birds and, remarkably, over 200 species of ants. It has a number of resident troupes of macaque monkeys and a wide range of other small mammals and snakes. Despite its relatively small size of less than 100 hectares it provides an impressive rainforest habitat in close proximity to the city. The dominant trees are in the dipterocarp family and include seraya, one of which is claimed to be 360 years old.[13] Located on the highest hill in Singapore, and rising no more than 163 metres, Bukit Timah nature reserve is an easily accessed location of outstanding ecological merit, good educational potential and aesthetically attractive landscape, and has demanding recreational facilities.

The interpretation centre was constructed in 1992 and comprises two rectangular blocks connected by an open walkway built on existing level formations of three-metre height difference. The front two-storey block houses the main exhibition space with rangers' accommodation above and services below. The rear, higher level block contains offices, a meeting room, a shop and toilets and is the only section that is air-conditioned. The overall design reflects the established vernacular architecture of colonial house construction in the Southeast Asia region and presents itself as a

modest, simple but harmonious structure built into the green backdrop of the primary forest habitat.

The generous overhangs to the roof, which have no gutters, permit the heavy rain to discharge directly to the natural slopes of the site and the surrounding natural environment provides good shading facilities. The lack of ceilings to the exhibition space permits the interesting roof structure to be enjoyed and creates sufficient air space to enhance the cooling effects of natural through-ventilation. Much of the remaining structure is open-sided enabling users to benefit from cross winds. Generous open seating areas at both levels allow users to relax and enjoy the green environment of the nearby forest. A spacious terrace below the front section is used for evening dinners and outdoor slide presentations, to enable users to maximise their enjoyment of the natural setting.

The planting of native tree, fern and shrub species around the built structures provides additional real-life educational facilities.

The planting of native tree, fern and shrub species around the built structures provides additional real-life educational facilities and when fully grown will further enhance the aesthetic setting and provision of shade. The car park is set well below and away from the centre, thus enabling visitors to experience a vehicle-free and relaxing environment.

Sungei Buloh Nature Park Visitor Centre

Completed in 1993, this centre designed by Thomas Wong Kok Woh is located in the only protected wetland nature reserve in Singapore. Sungei Buloh comprises an area of 87 hectares of coastal habitat located in the northwest corner of the main island. It contains 40 hectares of prawn ponds enclosed by two small rivers and a 9.5 hectare offshore island of mangrove. There are six hectares of freshwater ponds and over 150 species of birds have been recorded here. The park caters mainly for migratory wading birds but also accommodates resident heron nesting-grounds. It is well provided with access trails along the original bunds constructed by prawn farmers and is amply supplied with low-level hides, boarded mangrove walks and two tower hides. All bunds are provided with adjustable sluice gates which are used to control the sea-water levels inside the ponds to ensure suitable conditions exist for wading birds. The main boarded-bridge access across the Sungei Buloh Besar (large bamboo river) conveniently provides both a physical and visual separation between the visitor centre itself, the main hide and the birds' roosting and feeding grounds.

The concept plan for the centre considered the intrinsic ecological habitat of the site and the development approach was to minimise the changes and disturbances to the site ecology.[14] The centre was sensitively designed to 'float' over a marsh area which was actually created underneath it, and comprises a series of one-storey timber-framed buildings interconnected by timber open-sided walkways. Attractive pitched roofs have extensive overhangs which discharge rain to the many vegetated open spaces between the buildings. The main entrance approach, across a small bridge leading to the main reception area, is particularly attractive with freshwater pond areas on either side edged by prolific diverse vegetation. The accommodation comprises a small theatre, research and administrative offices, workshops,

a shop and a restaurant. The larger areas comprise several exhibition spaces which are open with a number of viewing balconies to allow visitors to enjoy the closeness and beauty of the natural environment. The car park has been located well away from the centre and a timber walkway between the two provides the visitor with an interesting walk through the forest on arrival but minimises the environmental impact of trampling and compacting the ground.

high to the rear, the front appearance is one of low scale, with a modest car-parking slip road across the entrance. On entering the gate in an attractive granite stone wall, an interesting open-space courtyard containing two freshwater ponds and tropical vegetation is immediately visible. The layout as indicated on plan comprises three blocks which are interconnected with open communal areas by walkways. This important feature permits users to enjoy cross-wind ventilation whilst being adequately protected from the elements.

Southeast Asian vernacular architecture is a 'model of a building that has a tripartite entity comprising a base (or podium), a superstructure (post and beam timber construction) and a pitched roof (generous roof eaves)'.

Above and opposite
Cheah Kok Ming and Poon Hin Kong and the Public Works Department of Singapore; Institute of Southeast Asia Studies, Kent Ridge Campus, National University of Singapore, 1998.

Notes
1. Ian McHarg, *Design with Nature*, Natural History Press (New York), 1969, p 197.
2. Ken Yeang, *Designing with Nature. The Ecological Basis for Architectural Design*, McGraw Hill (New York), 1995, p 35.

Institute of Southeast Asia Studies, Kent Ridge Campus, National University of Singapore

This building houses researchers' offices, a library and various meeting and conference facilities and was constructed in 1998. It was conceived to meet the needs of Southeast Asian researchers and therefore has a strong cultural component in its conception. The design is somewhat unusual in comparison to most of the other faculty buildings at Kent Ridge. In the words of the architect, Cheah Kok Ming, it was 'inspired by principles that are well established in Balinese architecture'.[15] Although the building is six storeys

Only the study, meeting rooms and the library are fully enclosed and air-conditioned. Lim describes the Southeast Asian vernacular architecture as a 'model of a building that has a tripartite entity comprising a base (or podium), a superstructure (post and beam timber construction) and a pitched roof (generous roof eaves)'.[16] The buildings have been orientated so that the longest facades are on the north–south axis to minimise solar gain, and the much warmer east and west elevations are allocated to mechanical and electrical service rooms and staircases to serve as buffers to solar heat. The large spaces between the blocks are well vegetated and, because of the openness of the access ways, views of this internal landscaping are

3. McHarg, *op cit*, p 184.
4. Yeang, *op cit*, p 18.
5. Milton Pereira, 'Sustaining Our Cultural Heritage' at the Cities and Sustainability Conference, Sri Lanka, 2000.
6. Brace B Taylor, *Geoffrey Bawa*, Thames and Hudson (London), revised edition, 1995, p 9.
7. Robert Powell, *The Tropical Asian House*, Select Books (Singapore), 1996, p 15.
8. Ibid, p 13.
9. KS Tay, 'Towards an Ecologically Responsible Urban Architecture', *Singapore Institute of Architects Journal*, no 183 (Mar/April 1993), pp 49–51.
10. Ken Yeang, *Theory and Practice in Bioclimatic Skyscrapers*, Artemis (London), 1994, p 17.
11. M Hough, *Cities and Natural Process*, Routledge (London), 1995, p 1.
12. Wong Kok Woh, 'Bukit Timah Nature Reserve Interpretation Centre', *Singapore Institute of Architects Journal*, no [174] (Sept/Oct 1992), pp 48–9.
13. S Lum and I Sharp, *A View from the Summit. The story of Bukit Timah Nature Reserve*, Nanyang Technological University, Singapore, 1996.
14. SJ Chia and KW Woon, 'Sungei Buloh Nature Park', *Singapore Institute of Architects Journal*, no [174] (Sept/Oct, 1992), p 50.
15. V Lim, 'The Institute of Southeast Asia Studies', *Singapore Institute of Architects Journal*, no 200 (Oct/Dec 1998), [p 34].
16. Ibid, [p 38].
17. C Briffett and Marziah Omar M Bte HJ, 'Planning and Designing Developments Naturally', *Singapore Institute of Architects Journal*, no 187 (Nov/Dec 1994), pp 43–52.
18. Steven Owen, *Planning Settlements Naturally*, Packard Publishing (Chichester), 1989, p 128.

available throughout the entire building. This creates a sense of a building that harmonises itself with nature and maximises its aesthetic appeal, providing a tranquil experience that befits a place of study, learning and research.

Summary

This review has attempted to identify buildings in the highly urbanised country of Singapore that interact closely with nature and provide their users and visitors with experiences that are often lost in the normal 'concretisation' of cities. It can, of course, be argued that the success of such designs is highly dependent on their close proximity to existing natural settings and is more easily achieved where space is not at a premium and when economic factors do not predominate. It is also accepted that the dehumanisation of the environment caused by tall skyscrapers, and the lack of opportunity to plant and maintain trees and other vegetation in central city districts, will work against the desirable interaction of buildings with nature. Despite this, there are many opportunities to use the ideas discussed here in high-rise city constructions, as demonstrated by the work of Ken Yeang and Tay Kheng Soon. For example, the vast areas of flat roofs, balconies and podiums can be planted, vertical walls can be trellised and landscaped with climbers, open courtyards, light wells and ground spaces can be vegetated. The road and riverside corridors that are present in most cities can also provide many other opportunities to introduce nature in close proximity to buildings.

In Singapore today several projects are under way to provide an island-wide network of connecting parks, to configure green trails through the city and to cultivate roof vegetation in city districts to reduce heat-island effects and even to grow vegetables. This will enable city dwellers to enjoy the psychological, emotional, recreational, ecological and aesthetic benefits that nature can supply. Living in an equatorial climate provides many opportunities to make better use of natural assets since there is a relatively rich biodiversity and the potentially rapid growth of vegetation is attractive and easy to encourage. Over the years a lot of attention has been paid to greening the city and few other cities in Asia can match the number of trees and plants Singapore contains. Having achieved the garden city concept, what is now desired is to create a green city in a garden.

These case studies reinforce the point that we should start the design process by thinking about what already exists naturally and try to work in harmony with preserving that environment. What is sustainable is not generally that which is man-made, which is generally more expensive to maintain and requires continuous regeneration. On a site-specific basis there is a need to consider the retention of existing topography, freshwater areas and stream courses, and for conserving as much of the natural habitat and established ecosystems as possible.[17] A detailed consideration of the microclimatic conditions that will result from correctly orientating a building, from using trees and plants for shading and pollution filtering, and from protecting building interiors from heavy rains should be instituted. The creation of naturally ventilated spaces that can also be used as visual landscaped courtyards, as shown in the case studies, is also essential. Last but not least, a respect for culture that ensures a design is representative of a region rather than simply an international clone is needed, and an appreciation of nature from which all sources of life derive. As in much of the tropics, low-energy design is not the primary task of sustainability – it is merely part of a bigger picture of bioclimatic architecture.

As suggested by Steven Owen in *Planning Settlements Naturally*: 'The natural features of a place are its most endearing attributes.'[18] ◬

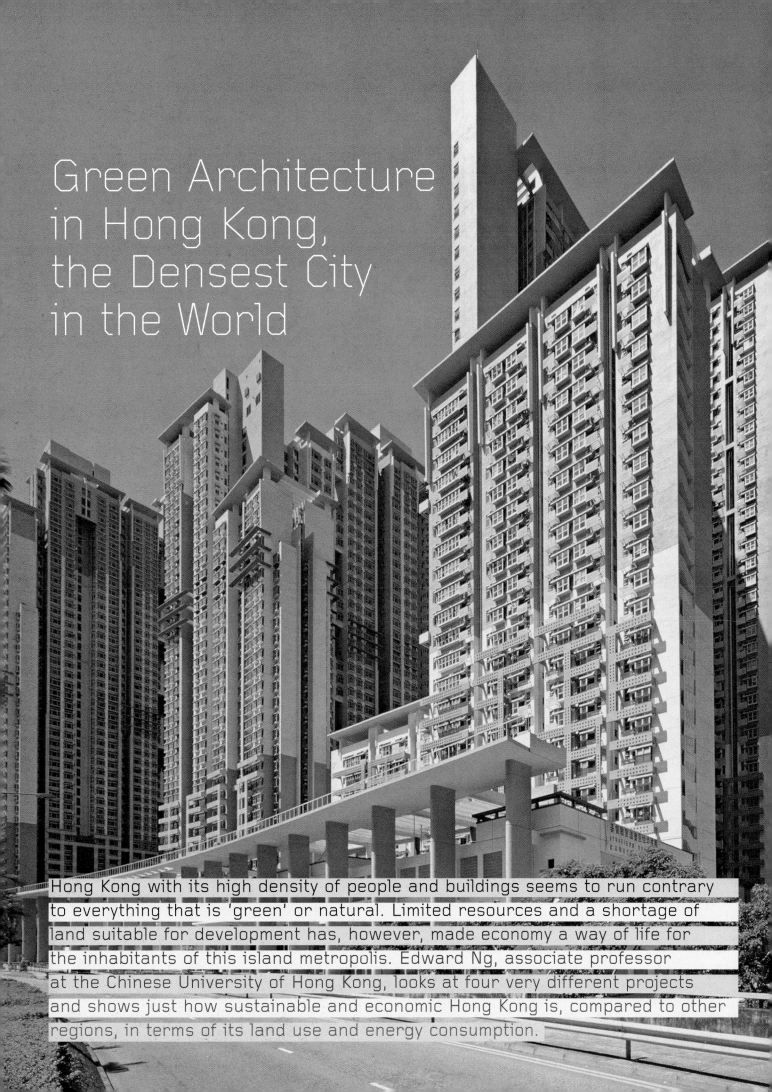

Green Architecture in Hong Kong, the Densest City in the World

Hong Kong with its high density of people and buildings seems to run contrary to everything that is 'green' or natural. Limited resources and a shortage of land suitable for development has, however, made economy a way of life for the inhabitants of this island metropolis. Edward Ng, associate professor at the Chinese University of Hong Kong, looks at four very different projects and shows just how sustainable and economic Hong Kong is, compared to other regions, in terms of its land use and energy consumption.

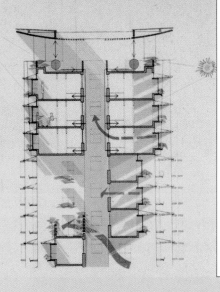

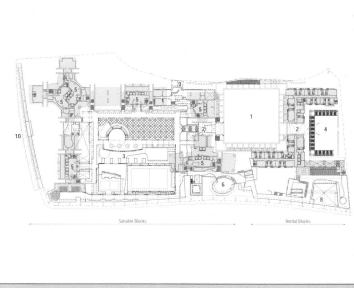

Rumour has it that when the Empress Dowager of the Ching dynasty was asked to cease sovereignty of 'an island' to the British Empire, she enquired of her eunuch, 'Where exactly is it?'. It was noted that she was a bit impatient when the map of the Chinese empire and the insignificant dot at its corner was shown. 'What are the British going to do with a barren piece of rock like that?' she questioned. 'And,' she added, 'I would like to make it a point that I should not be disturbed with such a minor request next time.' She could never have imagined that, 150 years on, this little 'rock' of 1,000 or so villagers would become a major Asian metropolis and earned itself a place as one of *National Geographic*'s 10 'must visit' places.

Hong Kong's climate is subtropical. For half the year, from October to March, it tends towards temperate with pleasant breezes, plenty of sunshine and a comfortable average temperature of 20°C. Occasional cold fronts from continental China can lower temperatures to below 10°C in urban areas, but nonetheless, these are the best months of the year. The other half of the year is hot and humid. Humidity of over 80 per cent and a daytime temperature that averages 28°C and rises to 34°C characterise the weather. From time to time during the summer months tropical cyclones bring heavy rain and high winds of 150 kilometres per hour or more. Environmentally, designing buildings for Hong Kong is not difficult. The strategy is to maximise natural ventilation, minimise solar heat gain and provide sturdy shelter from heavy topical rainstorms and cyclones.

Dealing with the environmental characteristics of Hong Kong is straightforward. However, attempts to classify this island metropolis according to any known social, cultural, urban or environmental theory has failed. As the locals say, 'There is only one Hong Kong, and it is impossible to find imitations'. In a nutshell, Hong Kong is located at the southern end of China. It is a collection of islands that

total 1,100 square kilometers and has a population of seven million people. Its economy is one-seventh of the United Kingdom's with a GNP of US$26,000 per capita. It boasts the world busiest container port and houses some of the world's most profitable enterprises. An airport the size of Gatwick and Heathrow combined has just been built on land completely reclaimed from the sea. Hong Kong is a jungle city of high rises. The foundations of the world's tallest building are being laid. And over 10 million visitors arrive each year, to marvel at all this. Yet, amidst all the hustle and bustle of the economy and international travel, Hong Kong also boasts a collection of country parks that cover almost 50 per cent of its land area. It houses one of Asia's most important wetland under the 1971 Ramsar Convention. It is also home to the 100 or so unique and endangered 'pink' dolphins. And, within its tight boundaries, it is still possible to find fishing villages and settlements which are almost untouched by the onslaught of civilisation.

Hong Kong is a land of paradoxes. It defies gravity and common sense – literally in that order for visitors who flew over the Kowloon city to land at the old Kai Tak Airport. Given the circumstances and the dilemma, how should one proceed to define green architecture in Hong Kong? If there is such a thing in an ultra-dense, ultra-compact metropolis, what is it? And how should it be critically understood? What shade of green could it be conveniently referenced to?

Hong Kong was a 'sustainable' city long before the term was used – or hijacked – by environmentalists. Since 1949, when the communists took over China, it has been a safe haven for economic and political emigrants from the mainland. Millions came here over a period of some 30 years, bringing nothing but a hope to 'ensure and sustain a quality of life'. This desire to survive and make a living has remained the spirit of Hong Kong until today. The city has no natural resources of its own. Apart from the air one breathes everything, including water, has to be imported. The gregarious and tolerant attitude of Hong Kong's average inhabitants can best be seen in the houses, or pigeonholes, they live in. Mass housing of unprecedented height and density is the norm. The newly constructed residential sites in the city's satellite

Opposite
Anthony Ng, Verbena Heights, Tseung Kwan O, 1997.

Above left
View of the main entrance foyer of Verbena Heights.

Above middle
Drawing outlining the concepts behind the environmental provisions at Verbena Heights.

Above right
The site plan of Verbena Heights.

towns are designed with a density of 2,000 to 2,500 inhabitants per hectare. If there is a Nobel Prize for the most efficient and effective use of land resources, Hong Kong will win hands down. Apartment blocks some 100 metres high are packed so closely together that the distance between them is a meagre 40 metres. To ensure that no valuable land is wasted, each block is built on top of a multistorey podium which houses all the amenities required to support the community. To service the towns, mass-transit railways are being built, cutting estates into manageable plots. Any land that is left over will be given to charitable organisations for school buildings and community centres. The crumbs will be collectively known as parks and leisure grounds. Hong Kong is a vision that all the world will need to share within a generation.

Verbena Heights, Tseung Kwan O

One of the many new towns that are taking shape is Tseung Kwan O on the east side of the old Kowloon peninsula. Part of the town was a landfill site until 18 years ago when massive land reclamation took place. Today Tseung Kwan O is thriving, with 250,000 inhabitants living in an area just under 600 hectares. In two years' time the mass-transit line will be completed and the town will continue to grow until the population reaches 500,000 to 600,000.

Situated at the heart of the town centre is the award-winning Verbena Heights designed by Anthony Ng. The development is reputed to be the first high-density housing in Hong Kong that took green and environmental issue seriously from day one. The architect states that:

The project represents an attempt to address environmental design concerns (energy minimisation, resources efficiency, water conservation, occupancy health and comfort) appropriate to the subtropical climate whilst

providing a high-density, high-rise housing design integrating with identity and delight for residents. Instead of the prevalent cruciform plan commonly adopted elsewhere in Hong Kong, an alternative thin linear layout is developed for the residential floors.

The linear blocks are planned around three elevated landscaped courtyards. Extensive wind-tunnel tests were conducted to maximise natural and cross ventilation at the ground and upper levels. The building height steps down towards the direction of the prevalent summer breeze. Multistorey mid-air balconies were devised to enhance wind permeability of the building mass. As a result, drastic improvements in air movement in and around the site have been achieved. So much so that windbreaks and canopies have to be employed at strategic positions to the wind climate at pedestrian level.

Solar and daylight studies went hand in hand with ventilation studies. External screens and light shelves were employed to provide effective shading as well as to enhance daylight in interior spaces. Vertical shading devices were preferred as they are less problematic in terms of maintenance and hygiene in high-rise living conditions. Low embodied energy and longer lasting and recycled materials were specified, and construction wastes were reduced by using reusable formworks.

The development is provided with a wide spectrum of community facilities at the ground and podium levels. Landscaped and covered walkways connect the blocks to each other, to other nodal points and to the nearby public transport interchange. The careful consideration of human scale, and spaces distributed at 'walking' intervals, ensures that it remains a pedestrian environment.

Hollywood Terrace, Western District

Whilst Verbena Heights consciously addressed the issue of environmentally-friendly design, another example of urban high-density housing, by Rocco Yim, approached the notion of sustainability more subtly. Hollywood

Above: left to right
View of Hollywood Terrace by Rocco Yim from Queen's Road Central.

Hollywood Terrace, Western District, 1998.

Plans highlighting the concepts behind the spatial layout (top), circulation (middle) and environmental provisions (bottom) of Hollywood Terrace.

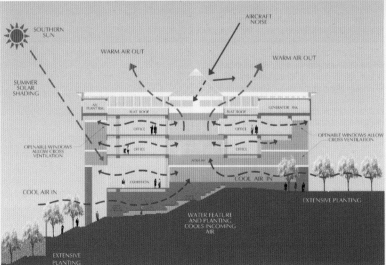

Top
Simon Kwan & Associates,
Jockey Club Environmental
Building, Kowloon Tong, 1996.
This view looks towards the
main entrance of the building.

Bottom
Drawing illustrating the
concepts behind the
environmental provisions
in the Jockey Club
Environmental Building.

Terrace is located at the heart of an old and established district in urban Hong Kong. The challenge was to respect, 'sustain' and complement the existing urban pattern of open space and traffic and circulation systems. Nesting through the development is a series of public landscaped terraces. Lifts and stairs form part of an elaborate and efficient route that links the two plateaus of the sloping site and allows 24-hour pedestrian access through it. The journey is a pleasant and surprising one, almost like an oasis and a maze combined. Environmental comfort has not been neglected. The apartments are configured so that they all face predominantly north and south – despite a very difficult site. Overlooking between apartments is effectively avoided, so occupants have the option of pulling back blinds for daylight. And, despite the small unit size, most living areas are capable of being cross-ventilated.

Both Verbena Heights and Hollywood Terrace were designed for the Hong Kong Housing Society – a provider of cheap and affordable housing. Little advanced technology or gadgets are employed but identity and dignity are provided through sustainable design.

Table 1
Energy Consumption and CO_2 Emission
– Hong Kong vs Other Key Industrialised Countries

Industrialised Nations

		Emission		Consumption	
	CO_2/capita Metric tonnes	CO_2 Kg/PPS $ of GDP	Kg of oil Equivalent/capita	$ GDP/Kg of oil equivalent
Hong Kong	3.7	0.2	1,931	12
China	2.8	1.0	902	0.7
Singapore	21.6	0.9	7,835	3.8
Japan	9.3	0.4	4,058	10.5
USA	20	0.7	8,051	3.4
UK	9.5	0.5	3,992	4.8

* 1997 data (source: *United Nations Statistics Yearbook*, 1997)

Jockey Club Environmental Building, Kowloon Tong

From the workers' perspective, social status and recognition can sometimes be attributed to the number of jobs a person holds, the hours he or she works and the number of calls they get on their mobile. These are accepted signs that someone is getting there. Recent surveys and polls suggest that workers and students in Hong Kong work longer hours than their counterparts in the rest of Asia. And whilst they were never too choosy about their work environment in the past, the demands of today's more discerning workforce provide an opportunity for local architects. Most of the time this means another expensively cladded high-rise tower, but with sustainable design, the office in Hong Kong changes its fundamentals.

Another significant project is the Jockey Club Environmental Building by Simon Kwan & Associates, completed in 1996. The building adapted the principles of traditional Chinese building typologies, technologies and methods to contemporary urban circumstances. According to Simon Kwan:

'If the cylindrical building form and its attendant fenestration refer, stylistically, to the traditional Hakka village fortress, then the decision to carve a public corridor through the building represents an interesting extension of this respective building typology. Two key insights apply. First, the permeable rendering of the building constitutes a signal of openness, optimism and confidence. Secondly, and perhaps more important, such a tactic complements and facilitates the building's environmental agenda.'[1]

The building has purity of form and planning. An open-air public corridor runs through it demarcating and defining the symbolic north–south axis of traditional Chinese architecture. An open atrium on the route provides ventilation and natural lighting to the surrounding office spaces and the transparent double-glazed atrium cap admits daylight whilst controlling heat gain. Smaller windows dominate the external facade. The solid east and west elevations need no additional help to shade the sun at this latitude. The recessed, but fully glazed, windows emphasise the circular form: the gesture is symbolic as well as environmental.

'The conscious act of place-making is intrinsically linked to the environmental features of the building,'[2] Simon Kwan revealed in a subsequent lecture. The interplay of inside and outside, the joy of light and shadow, solid and void, natural and artificial, and Yin and Yang has its genealogy in Chinese architecture and philosophy. To be this close to the remote heritage from which all these come is to acknowledge forces beyond the natural elements. If there is a hidden agenda, and if it has to be explained with the term sustainability, it

Notes
1. Simon Kwan & Associates Ltd/Architects Planners Designers, Project Portfolio: AD monograph: *Green and Sustainable Design in Hong Kong.*
2. *Ibid.*
3. *Ibid.*

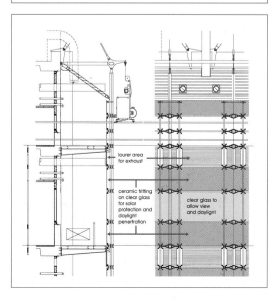

appears that the building is protraying it with poise and civility – almost like a mandarin. 'We search for solutions that elevate the pragmatic aspects of an architectural challenge, transform presumed constraints into engaging design and celebrate the refinement of necessity,'[3] Simon Kwan concluded.

Kadoorie Biological Science Building, Hong Kong University

In marked contrast to the Jockey Club Environmental Building, the Kadoorie Biological Science Building by Leigh & Orange Architects provides an elegantly innovative architectural solution for a highly technical building on a small and constrained site. The 10-storey building sitting on eight 10-metre-high upturned pyramidal columns contains eight floors of laboratories and one upper floor of aquariums and greenhouses. The east–west orientation of the site means the building's major facades will be exposed to long hours of solar heat gain. To the credit of the architects, the environmental challenge was conveniently translated into a powerful and yet effective architectural solution. The 'black box' laboratories were enveloped with a concrete enclosure and semiperforated outer curtain walls. They are set 2.5 metres apart and form external zones for services, maintenance and a filter to the external environment. The double-skin arrangement was designed to prevent solar gain and create a stack effect to take unwanted solar and equipment heat away. The result is a calculated reduction of 37 tonnes of CO_2 per year.

These four projects in Hong Kong may be unrelated in their inceptions. However, they all share common agendas such as: how the building addresses the land and the urban fabric around it; how it contributes to a matrix of movement and human needs; how the spaces are designed to be as dense and as flexible as possible to minimise the resources used; how sustainability can be developed in a hot, humid climate.

To evaluate these buildings in isolation according to the amount of energy used, the materials spent and the waste they produce is missing the point. In a dense built environment, it is not the building that matters. It is the collective whole of buildings, supporting human life with the minimum effort and maximum efficiency, that counts. Buildings in Hong Kong are compact, efficient, mostly mixed use and provided with well-planned amenities generally within walking distance. The various settlements are so compact that they can be served by a highly efficient and cost-effective public transport system (Table 1). The per capita energy consumption is low compared to cities of an equivalent size and economic standing. What is more important is that the energy has been very efficiently used to generate wealth and a material quality of living. This is the real measure of sustainable development in a high density metropolis. △

Top
Leigh & Orange Architects. The podium and the upturned pyramidal column bases of the Kadoorie Biological Science Building, Hong Kong University, 1999.

Middle
Drawing illustrating the concepts behind the environmental provisions in the Kadoorie Biological Science Building, Hong Kong University, 1999.

Bottom
Section and elevation of the double-skin glazing system of the Kadoorie Biological Science Building, Hong Kong University, 1999.

Thomas Herzog of Herzog and Partner

Green Questionnaire

What is your, or your practice's, definition of sustainable design?

Sustainability in architecture has to be regarded as one of the key issues of our profession, since almost half of the energy consumed in Europe is used to run buildings. A further 25 per cent is accounted for by traffic which – in part – is influenced by urban planners. The role of architecture as a responsible profession is of far-reaching significance in this respect. In this context, sustainable design can be defined as a working method, aimed at the preservation of our natural resources while using renewable forms of energy – especially solar energy – as extensively as possible.

What are your key concerns as a designer interested in sustainability?

There are various topics linked to the issue of sustainability, such as the choice and the provenance of materials, the energy needed for their transport and refinement, the process of construction, the degree of a building's thermal performance, expenditure for the operation and sustenance of buildings, their life span, flexibility with regard to the use, the adaptability of the building services, the suitability for assembly, dismantling and reassembling of the building components, and the possibility to convert or recycle. But one of the main issues is the integration of technologies and components to use renewable energies – especially solar energy – in a satisfying way, especially one that controls the impact on, and potential for, the appearance of the building.

How would you judge the success of a building in the 'green' age?

The success of a building is dependent on its overall performance, including its utility value, which has largely to do with the very complex topics that have been summarised under the term 'sustainable'. But the beauty and the design of a building is as important as its usability and function. Only beautifully made buildings contribute to our built environment in a sustainable way and will be regarded as worthwhile to be preserved. Here, the careful integration of technologies for the use of renewable energies offers the chance to generate new forms of architectural expression which are closely linked to the local condition, such as the microclimate and topography, the natural resources and the cultural heritage of a certain region.

In what way do you use nature as a guide?

In general I do not think that architecture can be deduced immediately from nature, since the design process and function of our buildings are quite different from what is found in most plants and animals. Nevertheless, there are a lot of lessons to be learnt from nature, especially with regard to the efficiency, performance, adaptability, variety and tremendous beauty which most organisms display under close observation. Considering that nature has to obey the same physical laws as man-made objects this should be seen as very encouraging for us, making it well worthwhile to study its principles and mechanisms. Δ

Above
Thomas Herzog

Right
High-rise administration building, Deutsche Messe AG, Hanover, 1999.

Opposite top left
Hall 26 of Deutsche Messe AG, Hanover.

Opposite top right
World Exhibition, Hanover 2000.

Opposite bottom
Detail of the roof structure at the World Exhibition, Hanover 2000.

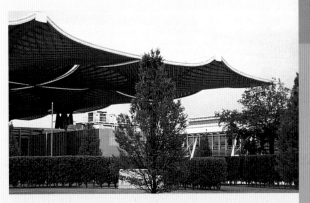

Sustainable Design in the Netherlands

Of all the countries and regions discussed, the Netherlands has the most mature approach to green construction. Ellen van Bueren, a research scientist at Delft University of Technology, and Chiel Boonstra, senior consultant of sustainable development at DHV Accommodation and Real Estate, Amersfoort, describe sustainability in terms of its evolution over the last 10 years and the key issues that have emerged. They have chosen three case studies which reflect these

In the past decade the Netherlands has seen many developments in sustainable design, characterised by a widening and deepening of the issue. Holistic, comprehensive approaches to design and construction are however still rare and many green design practices in the Netherlands concentrate on specific sustainability issues. This focus is commonly recognisable in the philosophy of a project and can sometimes even be recognised from the project's name. The City of the Sun, a new housing estate in the northern part of the country, where the use of sustainable energy has been the main aim, is a striking example of such naming and framing.

We have selected three projects with three very different green design philosophies, which should effectively outline the current state of affairs in the Netherlands.

The first is Nieuw Terbregge, a new housing estate in the city of Rotterdam. This project consists of about 1,000 new dwellings and a sports centre and is part of the immense task of building 500,000 new dwellings which the Dutch government committed itself to in the 1993 National Spatial Policy Plan. This plan states that the new estates have to be built between 1995 and 2005 and stipulates that green design knowledge is adopted when building the estates.

Unpopular postwar districts built in cities adjacent to the new estates suffer the consequences of these estates being realised. Those who can afford it, move to the new areas and rising unoccupancy rates are common problems in postwar districts. The housing companies and local governments in these districts have to take action and either renovate, or – and with the current extraordinary prices for land and housing this is often a more attractive option – demolish the buildings. Yet, the urban plans in most of these districts have some qualities which are worth preserving, and demolition produces huge amounts of waste.

Our project, De Componist (the composer), poses a highly innovative solution to these problems. When possible, the urban plans and buildings are reused. As a result, resource depletion and waste production are reduced by reusing the foundations and shells of former flats.

The Delft University of Technology Library is the third project we describe, and represents the wide body of knowledge about the greening of office buildings that has developed in recent years.

Introduction

Sustainable design in the Netherlands was started by volunteers and amateur architects in the 1970s. In the following decades the professionalisation of these small-scale initiatives was boosted by national government policies. The National Environmental Policy Plans (NEPPs) have been used to set the agenda for sustainable development and sustainable building in the Netherlands. Inspired by the Brundtland report, the first Dutch NEPP was published in 1989 and by 1990 its targets already needed to be updated. The revised edition came with an appendix entirely dedicated to sustainable construction, and from this moment onwards sustainable building became a popular issue for architects, urban planners and policy-makers. A large number of demonstration projects were initiated to prove the economic and technical feasibility of sustainable building measures, and to communicate these results to the building sector. The Ministry of Housing, Spatial Planning and the Environment produced three white papers, in 1995, 1997 and 1999, containing programmes and action plans to get sustainable building on the agenda of everyone involved in the built environment.[1]

Developments in Sustainable Design

The initial focus on sustainable construction with emphasis on the use of environmentally friendly materials, the reduction of construction waste, and energy efficiency and indoor climate has widened over the years.
• From materials and energy to other ecological themes. Themes such as water, traffic and transport, green structures and cultural heritage have become more important.
• From the construction and building level to the building block, neighbourhood and district level. Opportunities for sustainable building can be facilitated or frustrated at higher spatial scales.
• From newly built dwellings and offices to existing buildings. In the past decade the design of, and technologies for, newly built dwellings and offices have been improved and optimised. Attention has shifted to existing stock, and policy-makers have become aware that most of our future stock has already been built, and that it is in this existing stock that a considerable part of the environmental load is caused and important sustainability gains can be made.
• From a focus on one point in time to a life-cycle approach. The built environment consists of many elements with varying life spans. The environmental load of the elements within the built environment should be considered from 'cradle to grave', including the load caused during use and maintenance of the built environment. This life-cycle approach is now the basis for comparison between different materials, products and designs.

Above left
Active and passive solar
systems have been used at
Nieuw Terbregge.

Above right
A heat delivery station has
been integrated into the design
at Nieuw Terbregge.

Opposite left
Small-scale heat- and power-
units at Nieuw Terbregge
minimise the length
of transportation pipes.

Opposite right
Urban plan for De Componist,
Maassluis. The first phase of
the renovation work, described
here, will be completed in
December 2001. A second
phase is planned for
completion in June 2002.

• From the physical system to the social system. The social environment in which sustainable building takes place has become important. There is no ecological sustainability without social sustainability. Issues such as social segregation and quality of life have acquired a prominent place on the agendas of politicians and designers. The more issues and themes are addressed as sustainable building, the more the people responsible for these issues have to be involved in the project.

• From professionals to end-users. At the beginning of the 1990s sustainable building policies were focused mainly on professionals like architects, planners, installation experts, builders, contractors, etc. During the evaluation of the first demonstration projects it became clear that the behaviour of the end-users of the buildings was an important factor in the failure or success of sustainable building measures. Energy- and water-saving systems, for example, require disciplined behaviour by the occupants of buildings. When it comes to refurbishment, renovation, restructuring or reuse of existing buildings or neighbourhoods, the existing occupants cannot be ignored during the planning and carrying out of such projects.

Over time our knowledge has deepened on all the issues addressed by the concept of sustainable building. We have learnt about the effects of our actions on the environment, tools have been developed to measure these effects and methods have been introduced to weigh them. Many decision-support tools have been developed to help the decision-makers incorporate sustainability goals in their designs and decisions. Many technological innovations, ranging from high tech to low tech, have been developed to reduce the environmental load of creating, using and maintaining the built environment.

Key Influences: Water And Energy
The key issues addressed in Dutch sustainable building policies can be explained by a combination of geographic, climatic and, perhaps more importantly, cultural factors.

The Netherlands, part of the Low Countries, has to struggle to exist. About 50 per cent of the land is below sea level, and if it were not for our dykes, artificial dams and waterworks, the country would not exist in its current form. The polycentred Randstad, with six million inhabitants, is the cultural, economic and political centre of the Netherlands. This densely populated area is located in the western part of the country, the part which is below sea level.

Alongside energy, which has been an important sustainable building issue since the energy crisis in the 1970s, water is one of the key issues in sustainable building. Water quantity and water quality are addressed in sustainable building measures. Water quantity is concerned with both flooding and drought. Despite our huge amounts of surface water, the lowering level of our ground water is one of the biggest environmental problems in the Netherlands. The quality of our water is also of concern. Toxicants from many diverse sources pollute the ground, surface water and soils. The ecological value of the surface water, in terms of biodiversity, is in decline. Many water measures are therefore aimed at simultaneously addressing these various water problems. At the water-systems level, efforts are focused on keeping the water within the area – preventing its transportation to other areas with other water qualities – and directly infiltrating storm water to relieve the sewage system. At the building level, water measures are aimed at the reduction of water usage – for example, by installing water-saving taps and toilets – and by the reuse of grey water which is increasingly recycled and cleaned in filters.

For designers, water is an attractive sustainability issue. Living near water is popular in Holland, which gives designers freedom to design with water. IJburg, a new Amsterdam suburb which is now being built beside a lake, is one of the latest examples of giving water priority both as a design quality (such as the replication of Amsterdam-style canals with houseboats and docks for yachts) and as a sustainability quality. An integrated system of water infrastructure will embrace drinking water, grey water and water recycling using helofyten filters and ecological banks.

Key Players
Achieving sustainability goals in architecture and urban planning requires many political skills.

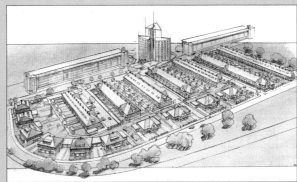

Decision-making in the Netherlands is characterised by consultation and consensus. Incorporating sustainability goals within building projects is also characterised by the process of wheeling and dealing, especially because most of the sustainability measures are not imposed by law, and their implementation therefore relies for a large part on the enthusiasm of the people involved. The architect and urban planner play important roles in the planning process, sometimes backed up by local government departments or by the project commissioner. Those who are successful are therefore equipped with both design and communication skills. They also have to be process managers, able to manage the stakeholders towards agreement on the plan to hand. Many sustainability measures require highly specialised knowledge which is beyond the capacities of individual designers. The designer should therefore bring together expert knowledge – technological knowledge and knowledge of the behaviour and preferences of the occupants or end-users of the buildings and public space – and integrate this in the design. Therefore, the most difficult challenge today for designers in the Netherlands is to find a balance between design qualities, sustainability goals and social goals. The three projects described below give a good impression of how Dutch designers deal with this challenge.

Nieuw Terbregge, Rotterdam

The RE-Start Rotterdam project, Nieuw Terbregge, demonstrates how innovation can be achieved at the scale of the development of an area of 860 houses. The RE-Start project involves eight European cities and addresses Renewable Energy Strategies and Technology Applications for Regenerating Towns. The project is used as an example of the houses Rotterdam plans to build in the near future.[2]

Nieuw Terbregge is innovative in the application of energy technology on a large scale and in the process this involves. The development of the entire project of 860 houses is in the hands of a commercial project developer, who

is working on the basis of performance requirements provided by, and agreed with, the City of Rotterdam.

The public/private partnership has made it possible to integrate the urban and architectural design of various parts of Nieuw Terbregge. Four architects have developed parts of the estate, and one of them is also in charge of the urban development. The energy strategies are seen as an integral part of the urban and architectural design and consist of:

Nieuw Terbregge is separated from a major highway by a hill made of controlled polluted sand. This has been developed into a linear park, from which one can overlook the highway and the buildings. On its north border Nieuw Terbregge faces the dykes of Rotterdam's river, the Rotte.

Part of Nieuw Terbregge demonstrates the application of solar energy in buildings. As the aim was to focus on replicable technologies, passive solar and active solar thermal systems have been used. Two-storey sunspaces on the entrance facade of the houses and 6-square-metre solar collectors contribute to the energy demand of space heating and domestic hot water.

Other parts of Nieuw Terbregge demonstrate integrating heat delivery by using small-scale, combined heat- and power-stations. Each heat delivery station provides heat to about 40 houses, thereby minimising the length of transportation pipes. Several solutions for planning and design integration are demonstrated in Nieuw Terbregge, Rotterdam.

Small-scale combined heat and power (chp) units are placed 'in cascade', so that the heat load is optimised. Heat is stored temporarily in a central storage tank. Electricity enters the electricity grid, and is partly used on site. One heat delivery station also contains a ground-water heat pump system. Combinations of heat/power installations and heat pumps are especially efficient and the heat/power installation produces electricity that can be used for the heat pump. The heat delivery stations are developed, managed and maintained by a utility company.

High-insulating glass (U-value of 1.0 W/m2K) and appropriate insulation levels (U-values below 0.3 W/m2K) have been used to minimise heat demand in the homes. The City of Rotterdam required the project to meet the requirements for its sustainable building programme. The choice of sustainable building materials has been a significant design input. The Dutch building code has contained an energy

performance standard for new houses since 1996. In 1998 and again in 2000 the maximum coefficient admitted was reduced. The RE-Start project, developed in 1996, demonstrated energy performances below the anticipated year 2000 level. The measures taken have reduced the emission of CO_2 by 25 (in 1998), to 55 per cent (in 2000), compared to new houses built in 1996. Further reduced levels are anticipated for the second part of Nieuw Terbregge, which is currently under development. The developer has found that the project is commercially valid. The policy to use urban, architectural and technical quality as a benchmark has allowed the integration
of energy issues. New project initiatives are already building on the experiences gained with the RE-Start Rotterdam project.

De Componist Maassluis

The Housing Corporation Maassluis (WSM) undertook an innovative and challenging project: how to transform and upgrade a 50-year-old housing estate to current standards of living? This challenge included the reuse of multistoreyed apartment buildings and the recycling of building components taken from such buildings. The apartments, built in the 1950s, no longer met the requirements for current standards of living. They were small, badly insulated and badly soundproofed with considerable problems with noise from neighbours. The neighbourhood consisted only of multistoreyed flats and, on the whole, offered an unpleasant living environment. Taking note of a rising unoccupancy rate, the WSM decided to restructure the neighbourhood. Instead of demolishing the building blocks and rebuilding new dwellings, the housing company decided to reuse the urban plan, to reuse some of the flats and to dismantle other flats and reuse their components and foundation to keep the demolition and construction waste produced by the project as low as possible. Reuse of the foundations and shells was expected to save eight to 10 per cent of the costs as well as minimise resource impacts.

De Componist, which formerly consisted of six apartment blocks, four storeys high, was transformed into 118 family unit dwellings and 41 apartments, all for sale. Two of the building blocks were renovated and fifth floors were added. The two top floors were removed from three other blocks and in these the remaining floors were redesigned as dwellings for families. The sixth apartment building was demolished to ground level and the foundation was reused for family dwellings.

Van de Seijp of Kokon Architects, the architect of this project, found the many constraints within which the design had to be made a challenge. It had to fit the existing layout of the buildings, which meant that the new apartments had to be designed with two load-bearing compartments, one 3.3 metres wide and one 4.5 metres. This provided the opportunity to design dwellings of various and exceptional widths, and resulted in a wide variety of dwelling typologies for different market segments. The challenge was to mask these differences, and was met by using a rather anonymous facade.

Dismantling buildings is not easy because most buildings are not designed with the idea of deconstructing and reusing various elements and components. In Maassluis the building team was faced with some difficult problems.[3] Many of the buildings were not constructed according to the plan on file, which made it necessary to introduce further safety measures. Furthermore, appropriate dismantling techniques did not exist so it was necessary to learn by trial and error. Another obstacle to reuse is the change in building regulations, which means that components used by the construction industry 50 years ago do not conform to present standards.

It was not possible to overcome these barriers within the planning of this project, and the building team had to give up their ambition to reuse building elements. However, they did succeed in reusing the urban plan, the foundations and the shells and the housing company therefore calls this project – which will be finished in December 2001 – a success and worth replicating in the future. If the cost of dumping building and demolition waste rises, the pressure for further innovations in this field is expected to grow.

The third project is the Delft University of Technology Library: a building of glass and grass. The Delft

Above left
The blocks of De Componist were designed with anonymous facades to mask the different widths of the various dwellings.

Above right
The glass climate facade of Delft University of Technology Library.

Opposite
The interior of Delft University of Technology.

University of Technology buildings have been relocated to a campus on the fringe of the city since the 1960s. The library, previously located in the city centre, moved there in 1998. The new library is located on the edge of the campus, behind the colossal Aula designed by Van den Broek & Bakema.

Like almost all university buildings in Delft, the Aula is a huge construction in concrete and it evokes associations with giant frogs, concrete thunderbirds or spaceships.[4]

Mecanoo Architects, the architectural company commissioned to design the new library, was started several years ago by Delft alumni. They decided that the Aula required a contrasting volume that would contribute to a campus atmosphere and provide a green landscape rising gently upwards at the rear of the Aula to continue as the library's triangular grass roof. The facades of the library are made of glass, strengthening the illusion of a hovering carpet of grass. The concrete paths that crisscross the landscape on the library roof are designed to invite students and academics to wander and linger informally. A cone of steel and glass pierces the grass roof. The cone symbolises technique, but is also functional: it contains reading cubicles and fills them with daylight.[5]

The climatic facade, the grass roof and the cooling strategy are the most important sustainability measures in the library design.[6] The required transparency is achieved by using glass climate-responsive facades. These maximise the use of daylight and save the energy needed for artificial lighting. The grass roof, of course, contributes to the architectural look of the library, but also has great heat-accumulating and insulating properties, so the space beneath it, where many books are stored, is less susceptible to changes in temperature. It also contributes to excellent soundproofing and to the infiltration and retention of storm water.[7] Hot and cold storage, another sustainable technique, avoids using disfiguring cooling units on top of the grass roof. Cold or heat captured in water is stored in two separate tubes in the ground in a sand layer which lies at a depth of 45 metres to 70 metres. In wintertime the warm water is pumped up to cool off in the open air in the library and is then pumped back into the other tube. In summer the water takes the opposite route.[8]

The decision-making processes that led to the design and realisation of the building were important in this project. From the beginning of the design process in 1993, the university board decided that the library should be 'green', both architecturally and technically. BOOM, a consultancy company that specialises in environmental design, was added to the team to maximise the greening of the design. The hot and cold storage, which fitted perfectly in the architectural design, was one of their concepts. Other ideas, such as solar panels and a special green galvanising process for the steel construction, met with more resistance, either because they were too expensive or because their technical feasibility was doubted.

However, this project, like many other innovative sustainable buildings, has had its problems. The grass roof shows that new combinations of materials and techniques can lead to difficulties that can not always be foreseen and prevented. The methods that were used turned out to be insufficiently waterproof and today state-of-the art sustainable building prescribes other construction techniques for grass roofs. Realisation of the project turned out to be another problem. The design required very precise implementation and the choice of intelligent building systems was not always the best from a sustainability point of view.

The Delft University Library opened its doors to users in 1998 and despite the teething troubles, which seem to be almost inevitable with ground-breaking techniques, the library fulfils expectations. It is a building which challenges students and academics to study and to debate and confirms the importance of practice in the Netherlands to the wider understanding of sustainability. △

Notes
1. HR Haarman, EN van Leeuwen and MAR de Haan, 'Sustainable Building Policy in the Netherlands', Milieu, *Journal of Environmental Sciences,* special issue: Sustainable Building in the Netherlands, no 2 (2000), pp 62–70.
2. City of Rotterdam and Proper Stok Dwellings Ltd, Nieuw Terbregge. Duurzaam Mooi aan de Rotte, 1998 (in Dutch, with English summary).
3. M Segers, 'Slopen en weer opbouwen. Maassluis tovert flats om in rijtjeshuizen', *Delta,* weekly magazine of Delft University of Technology, vol 32, no 31 (Oct 2000); and BJ Te Dorsthorst, T Kowalczyk, ChF Hendriks and J Kristinsson 'From Grave to Cradle: Reincarnation of Building Materials', Sustainable Building: Proceedings of the Maastricht Conference 22–25 October 2000 (Oct 2000), pp 128–31.
4. Mecanoo Architects, Delft University of Technology Library, *010 Publishers* (Rotterdam), 2000.
5. Ibid.
6. G de Vries and C Bouwens, 'Delft, Bibliotheek Technische Universiteit', *Duurzaam Bouwen,* no 2 (Feb 1998), pp 40–43.
7. E Koster 'Over de architectuur: de grasmat als verbindend element', *Duurzaam Bouwen,* no 2 (Feb 1998), pp 42–43.
8. Mecanoo Architects, *op cit.*

With special thanks to F van de Seijp of Kokon Architects and H van der Ploeg of WSM for their information and comments on De Componist. The authors would like to thank Mecanoo Architects for their contribution to the case study of Delft University of Technology Library.

Green Architecture in North America

As one of the greatest guzzlers of natural resources and energy, North America, particularly the United States, is often cast as the bad boy of global environmentalism. Brian Carter, Professor of Architecture at the University of Michigan, describes how the dominance of the private car, suburbia and market forces, combined with a lack of political will, have given sustainability little leeway in North America. He, however, describes five buildings in the United States and Canada whose sensitivity offers hope for the future.

Opposite
Bruder DWL Architects,
Phoenix Central Library, 1995.
Located on Phoenix's Central
Avenue, the library has an
exterior palette of concrete,
copper, stainless steel and
glass. The flat panelled copper
skins of the east and west
elevations, with the patina of
an old penny, are evocative of
Arizona's geological mesas
and the city's agricultural
heritage.

Above
'Shade sails' on the northern
elevation of the Phoenix
Central Library eliminate the
harsh glare of the summer
sun.

In North America the well-developed industrialised societies of the richest and most powerful countries in the world have advanced in ways that put into question many of the presumed determinants of architectural form. In the United States, for example, land has been settled and abandoned with impunity, climates have been readily modified artificially and building types, along with materials and constructional techniques, have been enthusiastically imported and invented.

In this context the conservation of natural resources has not been a primary concern. The combination of available space and a seemingly natural restlessness, together with the provision of an extensive road network and inexpensive fuel, has encouraged the spread of low-density development. The suburb has been prioritised over the city and the private car preferred over public transport. And although there have been some signs that suggest an increasing awareness of the need to conserve resources, recent discussions regarding the implementation of the Kyoto Protocol suggest that in North America this awareness is not necessarily supported by political will.

The Landscape Legacy and the Crisis of Contamination

During the 1970s landscape architects and designers like Ian McHarg and Lawrence Halprin sought to establish an understanding of the value of land and how new development could be planned to respect ecological patterns. More recently other designers have focused on the potential of new high-density, mixed-use developments to maximise the use of public transport and respect ecological systems. Peter Calthorpe has developed integrated proposals for sites in California – at Laguna West in Sacramento – and in Washington and Florida. Other schemes, like those by advocates of 'new urbanism', have been planned to create compact new communities in towns like Seaside, Celebration and Windsor in Florida. But in North America, where market forces predominate, the commitment to low-density development and single-use zoning continues to encourage the aggressive use of land and resources.

The development of industry on a large scale in America also created extensive sites where systems and processes of production frequently despoil the land. Many of these brown-field sites, defined by the Environmental Protection Agency (EPA) to include abandoned, idle or underused industrial and commercial properties where redevelopment is complicated by 'real or perceived' contamination, are located in cities. The Natural Resources Defence Council, one of the country's premier environmental groups, has suggested that there are 400,000 seriously polluted brown-field sites nationwide that need radical and extensive treatment to restore them to use. While funding is available through federal agencies and the EPA, much of the responsibility for brown-field development has shifted to state and local government. Many of these sites are located in the Midwest – America's former industrial heartland – where land reclamation projects have included the redevelopment of former steel mills on the Monongahela River to create the new Pittsburgh Technology Centre. One of the most significant current projects is in Detroit – the birthplace of the car industry. The state of Michigan first passed progressive brown-field legislation in 1990 and more recent modifications have helped to encourage the reuse of former industrial sites. Currently the Ford Motor Company is working with the architect William McDonough and landscape architect Julie Bargman to develop a plan to restore the 1,100-acre industrial site that was first developed in the flood plain of the River Rouge by Henry Ford and architect Albert Kahn in 1917. This has begun with a $2 billion scheme to build a new automobile plant on a 550-acre reclaimed brown-field site – a scheme that has been described as the largest industrial ecology effort in the world.[1] So there are signs that recycling, at least of land, is being taken seriously in the USA.

Low-Energy Design

Although inhibited by the availability of cheap fuel, there have been some efforts to utilise alternative energy sources. Initiatives to use passive solar systems have created modest benefits whilst other federal tax incentives have been designed to promote the use of wind power over more polluting fuels in America. Wind farms have been operational in California for several years and a new $16 million project was completed recently in Madison, New York. Energy from these sources, together with planned developments in Texas and the Great Plains, have prompted the US Energy Department to predict that 4,600 megawatts of wind power (enough to provide for 1.7 million households and almost double today's figures) will be available in 2001. The US Energy Secretary has set a goal of increasing wind's share of America's electoral capacity to 5 per cent by 2020.

Less stringent legislation and a tendency to amortise buildings over shorter periods has made the design of energy-efficient buildings develop more slowly in America than in Europe. Legislative initiatives, like Title 24 which was introduced to reduce energy use primarily by limiting the extent of glazing in new buildings, have been effective for several years in California. These have been strengthened more recently with the adoption of ASHRAE 90.1 as the standard to which the design of all federal government projects should comply. The Leadership in Energy and Environmental Design programme (LEED) released by the US Green Building Council in 2000[2] provides a performance-based assessment which embraces a wide range of concerns including site development, specifications for materials and the design of buildings to give both qualitative and quantitative measures to assess 'greenness'. Like the British Research Establishment Environmental Assessment Method in the UK, LEED is voluntary and its success depends on committed clients. However, it is becoming increasingly used and in Seattle all state-funded projects now have to produce a LEED assessment. These initiatives are helping to create better understandings of 'green' building and establish useful benchmarks for both clients and architects.

The power and capacity of industry has tended to limit awareness and innovation in the design of 'green' buildings in North America. After 1945 the design of many modern buildings was inspired by material research and product development prompted by the transfer of technology and production systems developed for the war effort. However, as the large corporations that supply the construction industry have sought to standardise in order to achieve increased efficiencies and maximise profits, much of that invention has been smothered. As these standardised ranges of industrial products are also made widely available through the extraordinary effectiveness of transcontinental distribution systems, new buildings tend to become generalised and overengineered. These characteristics are in sharp contrast to the particularity which is often required of 'green' buildings – buildings designed to respond to the characteristics of region and site, to specific uses and the long-term needs of a community, the nation and a global constituency.

Extreme Climates – A Mixed Blessing

Extremes of climate place stringent demands on designers in North America. For example, the use of natural ventilation, either to replace air conditioning or integrated with mechanical systems in 'mixed mode' schemes, is more successful in moderate climates. Consequently its use has been limited, with the most use in buildings along the West Coast. However, research has shown that certain building types can benefit from natural ventilation. So, for example, in

designing the new David L Lawrence Convention Center in Pittsburgh, Rafael Viñoly has explored the use of natural ventilation especially during those times when exhibitions are assembled or dismantled and when comfort needs are less stringent.[3] By contrast, the new computer science facility at York University in Toronto has been designed by Van Nostrand and Di Castri Architects in a joint venture with Peter Busby and Associates to create distinct zones of different uses, so as to incorporate natural ventilation as part of a mixed-mode system.[4]

Phoenix Central Library

Some of the most innovative and experimental initiatives have been prompted by architects designing buildings in extreme climates. The Phoenix Central Library in Arizona, designed by Will Bruder, is a large new public building in the centre of the sixth largest city in the United States. Phoenix is growing rapidly and has a population of well over a million. The city also extends over an area of 2,000 square miles. In designing the 280,000-square-foot library in this setting, the ambition was to create a building that emphasised a commitment to civic values and reflected concerns for sustainability.

Consequently the library was located on a downtown site, funded with money raised through the passing of a public bond issue, and was planned to provide for a broad range of facilities and programmes. It has also developed other concepts of 'greenness' through its integrative design approach which helps to address the extreme climate. The building has been organised with all the cloakrooms, staircases and plant rooms planned in two long 'saddlebags' to either side of a large rectangular five-storey library. As well as providing lateral bracing for the building, these saddlebags have been designed to shade the east and west facades from the hot desert sun. And, while the north and south facades are fully glazed to provide good levels of natural lighting within the library, they are also protected by external sun screens that use either fabric sails or adjustable louvres.

In developing the design, the architect explored the economies offered by industrialised construction. Consequently the main body of the building was designed to utilise readily available precast concrete components. Although precast concrete is more commonly used for warehouses and car-parking structures, Bruder saw it as 'a late 20th century vernacular material in the southwest'.[5] By adopting this material and benefiting from already perfected systems, he was able to ensure that the library was constructed

quickly and inexpensively. It also embodies
thermal mass that benefits long-term
performance and running costs. The library has
been planned with a large public reading room
on the top floor above four floors of stacks.
Inspired by Labrouste's Bibliothèque Nationale,
the structural system and constructional logic of
this generous double-height space are made
clearly legible. The room is also well lit, using
carefully controlled natural daylight, and has
good views out over the city. The library was built
with a modest budget – $98 per square foot –
and reflects a refined sense of economy. When
Bruder talks about the building he frequently
quotes Antoine de Saint-Exupery, the poet,
aviator and confidant of Le Corbusier, who said
that, 'in anything at all, perfection is finally
attained not when there is no longer anything to
add, but when there is no longer anything to take
away'.[6] This insight fittingly summarises the
design of one of the most significant and
environmentally sensitive buildings to be built in
America in the last decade.

Sandra Day O'Connor United States Courthouse, Phoenix

The Sandra Day O'Connor Courthouse, which is also in
Phoenix, opened in October 2000. It was designed by
Richard Meier as a part of the US General Services
Administration's Design Excellence Program – an
initiative to create a legacy of outstanding public
buildings. Like the Central Library it has been built on a
site in the heart of the city in an effort to anchor the
downtown of this otherwise overwhelmingly suburban
conurbation. The 571,000-square-foot courthouse,
together with a newly created plaza, fill a two-block
site and are part of a group of buildings that include the
City Hall, County Offices and the State Supreme Court.
Planned within a compact rectangular envelope, the
long facade of the new building, which fronts on to
Washington Street, opens on to an atrium. It is 350 feet
long and 150 feet wide and extends the public space of
the entry plaza into the courthouse. Described by Meier
as 'a great civic hall ... an inspiring space that belongs
to the people and the city'[7] this new public room also
highlights an innovative response to the design of the
environment.

In a place where summer temperatures can reach 122°F, to design a building with a 58,000-square-foot glass-enclosed atrium would seem to be creating a problem. However, by working closely with mechanical engineers from Arup, the architects were able to develop a passive system which maintained comfort conditions by using integrated systems of 'evaporative cooling', natural ventilation, conditioned spill air and shading to create an environment that provides a high level of human comfort. Evaporative cooling utilises a fine mist which is sprayed across a current of warm dry air. As the water is absorbed, the air's humidity increases while its temperature decreases. In the design of this courthouse, outside air is pulled in at the top of the atrium's glass facade just below the roof. It moves across the atrium under the roof until it hits the sixth-floor wall of the courthouse block. Above the gallery at this level, nozzles spray the air with water. As this moisture is absorbed, the air not only cools down but also becomes heavier and descends to the atrium floor. Exhaust air from the enclosed courthouse

climate and programme, and the cultural patterns of a locality, this search highlights an interest in heterogeneity and one that carries with it an inherent interest in the economy and enlightened intuition of the vernacular. Consequently, Seabird Island School in the Fraser Valley in British Columbia, which was designed by the Patkaus for and with the Salish Indian Band, made use of indigenous materials so that the same community could also construct the building. That this project was one of a series initiated by government made it all the more potent. For the more recent Strawberry Vale School in Victoria, the Patkaus adopted more common construction practices, but the design was also carefully planned to mitigate the impact of construction on the site by capturing and cleaning the runoff water through selected planting regimes before it re-entered the ground water. The building was also designed to maximise natural light within the school and materials were selected to minimise embodied energy and toxicity.

The Revenue Canada Building in Surrey, British Columbia, which opened in 1998, was the result of a design/build competition with an emphasis on low life-cycle costs. The 11,150-square-metre office building,

A great civic hall, an inspiring space that belongs to the people and the city, this new public room also highlights an innovative response to the design of the environment.

spaces and overflow from the air-conditioned balconies provide additional cooling. To complete the cycle; the air flows back outside through openings located several feet above the ground floor. Exploiting this low-cost passive technology and utilising shading devices, the temperature on the floor of the atrium during hot summer days is generally about 20 degrees cooler than on the street, and for most of the year the atrium can be maintained at a comfortable 73°F degrees making a significant and much-needed habitable civic space in one of the hottest places in America.

The View from Canada
In Canada the climate is also extreme. However, the scale of projects and the design approaches often appear more modest. The approach of a number of Canadian practices, perhaps most notably seen in the work of the Patkaus, highlights a search for what they have described as 'found potential'. In each of their projects this represents a considered reaction against homogeneity. Based on a close scrutiny of site,

designed by Peter Busby & Associates, was planned on five levels with two bars of office space connected by a core of service spaces, meeting rooms and storage. Developed to advance green design principles, the offices were planned so that virtually all the workstations are no more than eight metres from natural light and openable windows. A raised floor is used to distribute air, power and communications from below. One hundred per cent fresh air is provided in large volume at low velocity and employees can control the location and velocity of supply air at each workstation. Curved glass sun screens fitted externally, internal light shelves and low-e glazing help to create an energy-efficient envelope. To avoid glare in the offices, artificial lighting is indirect with 70 per cent provided as uplighting while photosensors optimise internal lighting conditions automatically. Exposed concrete ceilings allow heat from occupants and equipment to be absorbed during the day by the thermal mass which is then purged overnight. This dynamic thermal storage has made it possible to reduce the mechanical equipment and associated maintenance costs, and enables the building to operate at 60–70 per cent below the targeted ASHRAE 90.1 level.

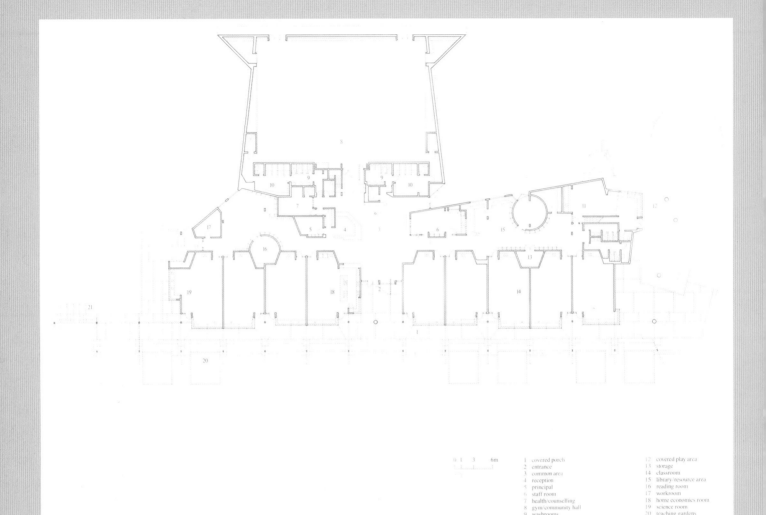

Top
Plan of John and Patricia
Patkau Architects' Seabird
Island School, British
Columbia, 1991.

Bottom left and right
John and Patricia Patkau
Architects, Seabird Island
School.

88

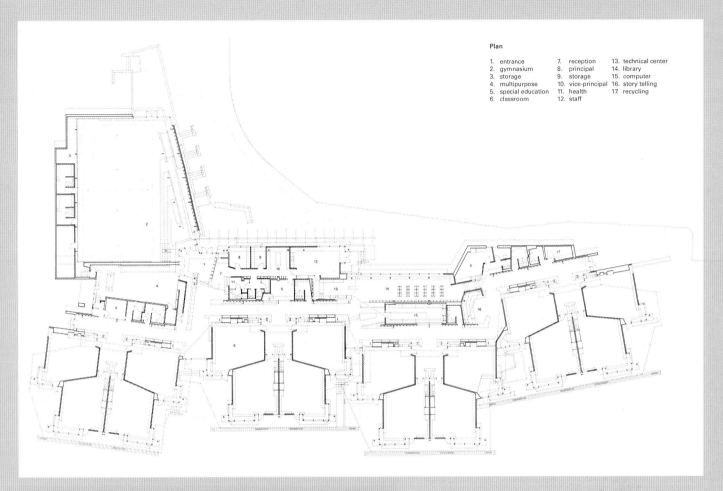

Plan

1. entrance
2. gymnasium
3. storage
4. multipurpose
5. special education
6. classroom
7. reception
8. principal
9. storage
10. vice-principal
11. health
12. staff
13. technical center
14. library
15. computer
16. story telling
17. recycling

Top
John and Patricia Patkau
Architects, plan of Strawberry
Vale School, Victoria, British
Columbia, 1996.

Bottom
Classrooms in the Stawberry
Vale School are planned so as
to overlook a woodland of rare
Garry Oaks.

Conclusions

Architecture in North America is gradually becoming 'green'. Progress reflects differences in America and Canada which originate out of societal priorities, economies and political preoccupations. However, one aspect which connects the work of architects seeking to advance ideas of a sustainable architecture in North America is that of patronage. Although it is relatively modest, some of the most significant recent work in both countries has been commissioned by the public sector. Secondly, whilst concerns for sustainability cannot yet be seen as truly transformative, they are influencing the work of established architects like Richard Meier. At the same time, smaller practices like McDonough, Will Bruder and the Patkaus are becoming more influential through an increasing amount of built work, successful competitions and invitations to practise across the continent. There are also signs that more collaborative work is bringing together architects, engineers and construction specialists. This is resulting in more integrative design solutions which benefit from increasingly sophisticated simulation techniques and software which provide designers with better tools to predict performance and particularise construction. It is in the searches for 'found potential', sponsored by inspired patronage and interdisciplinary design collaboration assisted by sophisticated technological expertise, that the greening of architecture resides in North America.

Right
Classrooms in the Stawberry Vale School are planned so as to overlook a woodland of rare Garry Oaks.

This page
An internal view of the glazed wall and of the entrance of Revenue Canada illustrate how an energy-efficient envelope was created with the the aid of curved glass sun screens on the exterior, internal light shelves and low-e glazing and internal loght shelves.

Notes

1. *New York Times*, 26 November 2000, p 50.
2. LEED Green Building Rating System, TM2.0 Ballot Version, US Green Building Council, January 2000.
3. Nadav Malin, 'What? No Air Conditioning in This Building, *Architectural Record*, May 2000), p 284.
4. *Ibid*, p 288.
5. Will Bruder, *Three Times Two* (1999 John Dinkeloo Memorial Lecture), University of Michigan: A Alfred Taubman College of Architecture and Urban Planning, 1999, pp 40–1.
6. *Ibid*, p 44.
7. Sandra Day O'Connor United States Courthouse, *US General Services Administration*, 2000, p 3.

Contributors Biographies

Chiel Boonstra is a Senior Consultant in Sustainable Development at DHV Accommodation and Real Estate, Amersfoort, the Netherlands.

Clive Briffett has a PhD in Planning and an MSc in Environmental Assessment and Management from Oxford Brookes University in the UK. He also has an MSc in Building Economics and Management from University College, London University, and is a Fellow of the Royal Institution of Chartered Surveyors and a member of the International Association of Impact Assessment. He is an Associate Professor in the Department of Real Estate of the School of Design and Environment, National University of Singapore. His books include *The Birds of Singapore* (Oxford University Press, 1993), and *Multiple Use Green Corridors in the City: Guidelines for Implementation* (Nature Society Singapore, 2000). He has edited proceedings for the Master Plan for the Conservation of Nature in Singapore (Nature Society Singapore, 1990), Environmental Issues in Development and Conservation (School of Building and Estate Management, 1993) and The State of the Natural Environment in Singapore (Nature Society Singapore, 1999). His current areas of research include the effectiveness of environmental assessment in Asia and the potential for strategic environmental assessment in East Asia. He has written for a wide range of international journals on matters relating to environmental impacts and management.

Brian Carter is the Chair of Architecture and a Professor of Architecture at the University of Michigan. An architect and urban designer, he was educated at the Nottingham School of Architecture and the University of Toronto. He has worked in practice, most recently with Arup Associates in London. In addition, he has taught at the University of Bristol, the University of California-Berkeley, the University of Liverpool, the Royal Academy of Copenhagen and the Rhode Island School of Design. An Associate of the Royal Institute of British Architects and a Fellow of the Royal Society of Arts, he has served the RIBA both as an external examiner and a juror in design competitions and awards. His writings have appeared in internationally published books and journals, including the *Architectural Review* and *Architecture*. Professor Carter has also curated a number of exhibitions, including the exhibit on the work of Royal Gold Medallist Peter Rice.

Chrisna du Plessis holds Bachelor and Master degrees of Architecture from the University of Pretoria. She lectured part-time at the university while pursuing a career as development strategist before moving in 1997 to the Division of Building and Construction Technology at the Council for Scientific and Industrial Research where she now works in the Programme for Sustainable Human Settlement. She is a member of two working groups dealing with sustainable development within the International Council for Research and Innovation in Building and Construction (CIB), and is joint co-ordinator of one of them (TG38: Urban Sustainability). In this capacity, she has written the South African report on sustainable development and the future of construction, and co-authored the chapter on urban sustainability in the CIB Agenda 21 for the Construction Industry. The CIB has recently appointed her to cordinate an Agenda 21 for Sustainable Construction in the Developing World. She is also a member of the Interim National Steering Committee on the implementation of LA21 and the Habitat Agenda for South Africa, and is involved in developing the country's National Strategy for Sustainable Development. She has delivered several papers at national and international conferences and workshops, and is the author of a number of internationally published papers and contributions to books on the subject of sustainable development.

Brian Edwards is an architect with a particular interest in sustainable design. He has practised and lectured widely in the UK and abroad, and has been a speaker on radio and television including BBC Radio 4's 'Costing the Earth'. He studied at the schools of architecture in Canterbury and Edinburgh and in Glasgow where he obtained his PhD. He is now Professor of Architecture at Edinburgh College of Art/Heriot-Watt University. He has also been Professor of Architecture at the University of Huddersfield. His other books include Green Buildings Pay and Sustainable Architecture.

Many of the ideas discussed in this issue are those raised at the RIBA's Sustainable Futures Committee upon which the guest editor sits.

Professor Lindsay Johnston is Dean of the Faculty of Architecture, Building and Design, the University of Newcastle, Australia. He is a former national councillor of the Royal Australian Institute of Architects and principal author of the RAIA Education Policy. He has been the recipient of a number of architecture awards for built works including the 1997 RAIA NSW Environment Award for an experimental 'autonomous' house and the 2000 RAIA NSW Premier's Award for tourist 'eco lodges'. He writes extensively on environmental architecture and his buildings have been published internationally.

Edward Ng is the Director of the Design Technology Laboratory and an Associate Professor at the Chinese University of Hong Kong. He was trained and qualified as an architect in the UK and obtained his PhD from Cambridge University. He has researched and published on daylighting design for high-rise cities, sustainable design of compact urban forms and green schools.

Ellen van Bueren is a Research Assistant in the Faculty of Policy and Management and DIOC The Ecological City at Delft University of Technology, the Netherlands.

94+ In the Realm of the Senses
Thomas Deckker

96+ Building Profile:
The Eden Project
Jeremy Melvin

101+ Practice Profile:
Zombory-Moldovan Moore
Helen Castle

109+ Book Reviews

110+ Highlights from Wiley-Academy

111+ Site Lines
Edwin Heathcote

In the Realm of the Senses

The recent publication in English of Oscar Niemeyer's autobiography *The Curves of Time* (Phaidon, 2000) has stimulated a new interest in the Brazilian architect Thomas Deckker. An English architect who has practised in Brazil, reflects on Niemeyer's career and his memoirs.

When the *Architectural Review* noted in 1954 that, 'to the European architect few creatures could look as fabulous as his Brazilian counterpart as he appears in the stories which filter back from Rio – of men with Cadillacs, supercharged hydroplanes, collections of modern art to make the galleries blush, bikini-clad receptionists and no visible assistants',[1] they must have had in mind one particular architect: Oscar Ribeiro de Almeida de Niemeyer Soares.

Niemeyer was born in 1907 into a patrician but modest family and brought up in Laranjeiras in Rio de Janeiro, a district of solid houses, with high-ceiling rooms and large gardens shaded by palm trees, that had hardly changed since the pictures of Debret. Niemeyer felt architecture to be a vocation. He studied at the Escola Nacional de Belas Artes and his time there included a year during Lucio Costa's short-lived 'Functional' course. Unwilling to compromise with current commercial architectural practice, upon his graduation in 1934 he became an assistant to Costa who, having himself converted to Modernism in 1930 was enduring five years with almost no work. It could not have been an easy decision for Niemeyer: Rio was then undergoing a boom, due equally to the programme of national self-sufficiency and to the Agache Plan for the reconstruction of the centre. It was, as Philip Goodwin, author of *Brazil Builds*, noted in 1942, part Paris and part Los Angeles. While architecture was conservative, engineering was very dynamic: the 'A Noite' building, where Costa had his office, was the tallest reinforced-concrete structure in the world in 1928. According to Costa, the young Niemeyer displayed no special aptitude for architecture.

Niemeyer learnt all he needed to know about the Modern architectural language in a few weeks in August 1936 during Le Corbusier's brief visit to Brazil as adviser on the new Ministry of Education building. Such was the confidence he gained that he was able to take the Corbusian formulation of Modernism and turn it into a highly sensual and urbane building that was immediately recognised as a masterpiece. He did this so successfully that Le Corbusier tried to claim it as his own: he doctored photographs and copied drawings sent to him by Costa after construction. While recognisably a Purist building, the concepts which made Niemeyer's work distinct from Le Corbusier's may be seen to have emerged here: the dynamic relationship of the forms to the urban space, the sensuousness of colour, the inhabitation of the ground space.

The story was repeated for the United Nations headquarters, New York, in 1947. Wallace Harrison had been impressed by the Brazilian Pavilion Niemeyer designed with Costa for the New York World's Fair of 1939, and invited him to join the rather mixed bag of consultants. Niemeyer provided the architectonic solution (model '32') to Harrison's preferred Modern aesthetic; the Beaux-Arts trained Harrison had no feeling for Modernism and of course later abandoned it for a monumental and authoritarian style. Le Corbusier had long abandoned his Purist style and would have preferred something like Chandigarh; sensing the battle was lost, he fiddled with Niemeyer's proposal to produce the unsatisfactory final solution (model '32-23').

Niemeyer encountered no such interference in Brazil, however. Gustavo Capanema, who had commissioned the Ministry of Education building, and Juscelino Kubitschek were deeply cultured and genuinely passionate about architecture. They were also ruthless technocrats, another factor which led Le Corbusier to believe that Brazil was an ideal country

for Modernism. Niemeyer became almost the court architect as Kubitschek, who commissioned Pampulha as mayor of Belo Horizonte, went on to commission Brasília as president of Brazil. Here, Niemeyer was able to repay his debt to Costa as he certainly recognised his hand in the five small pieces of paper he submitted for the competition for the urban plan.

Niemeyer relates that it was in his house in Canoas that Kubitschek became convinced that Brasília was feasible. It is possible, even probable, that Niemeyer then rushed to Juca's Bar in Copacabana, collected half a dozen friends and the barman, and that they drove 1,000 kilometres into the interior, only stopping to buy a lorry load of wood and hire a cook, and built the Catetinho Palace with their own hands. When Kubitschek dropped by in the presidential helicopter and found a little Niemeyer house, ready with cook and butler, how could he resist?

It becomes easier to understand the design of Brasília when one reads of the extraordinary trips across the totally unpopulated cerrado into the unknown interior of Brazil – 20 hours or more by car across dirt roads. The site was a desert of dry red silt; Costa, Niemeyer and Roberto Burle Marx made it bloom. Why should Brasília be like a normal city? Why not try to redeem the Modern covenant with landscape, which had been so disastrously grafted on to urban fabrics elsewhere?

The uncritical adhesion to Modernism was, of course, ultimately Niemeyer's – and Brazil's – undoing. The country's unresolved internal political conflicts brought about its downfall in a CIA-backed coup in 1964. Unlike so many Modern architects who paid lip service to political principles, Niemeyer was a genuine communist. His communism was expressed as a commitment to public service, fully in keeping with the technocratic ideals of his contemporaries. On the succession of the military government, Niemeyer went into a long and

necessary exile. He was fortunate to extend his career in France (the Communist Party headquarters, Paris, 1965; the Cultural Centre in Le Havre, 1972), Italy (the Mondadori headquarters, Milan, 1968) and Algeria (the University of Constantine, 1969). The military government was deposed in 1985, but the technocratic and meritocratic regime in Brazil which had supported Niemeyer had long disappeared. His latest works are rather an embarrassment: compare the Latin America Centre in São Paulo (1987) to the Praça do Três Poderes in Brasília (1960) or the Museum of Contemporary Art in Niterói (1997) to the project for the museum in Caracas (1954).

The reader need not look into The Curves of Time for any reflections on the demise of Modernism or any explanations of Niemeyer's career. The book is almost exclusively about his clients, friends and lovers, the beauties of Rio de Janeiro and the landscape of Brazil. In typically Brazilian fashion, saudades – the sense of fleeting happiness and past joy – permeates the book. Perhaps it is things like these, after all, which it is most important for an aged architect to reflect on. It may not matter that most readers will not know the personalities or the history: the true subject of the book lies in the realm of the senses. Δ

Thomas Deckker is the editor of The Modern City Revisited, Spon Press (London and New York), 2000, which includes his essay ' Brasília: City Versus Landscape'. Thomas Decker: Two Projects in Brasília' was published in Δ October 2000.

Notes
1. 'Report on Brazil', Architectural Review (Oct 1954), p 234.

The Eden Project

Like its greatest predecessors, the Crystal Palace and the Palm House at Kew, the Eden Project in Cornwall has captured the public's imagination. Here, Jeremy Melvin describes the design and engineering details of Nicholas Grimshaw's and Tony Hunt's magnificent lightweight domes which owe more to Buckminster Fuller than to the nineteenth century.

The geodesic dome is a perfect form for the Eden Project in Cornwall. The structure seems to take the familiar technology to new levels with its linked sequence of varyingly sized domes. So far these form two biomes that simulate warm temperate and humid tropical environments, showing that the famous structural system offers the lightness and economy the concept demanded. Also, the integrity of the idea that all the members are equally dependent on each other is an apt metaphor for the interdependence of the decisions that underlie the design. The resolution between the extremely complex ground engineering of an unstable china-clay pit and the predictable precision of the geodesic form finds a visual counterpart in the awkward problem of making an interface between two domes – here finessed by the sheer scale and the extraordinary nature of the contents.

The project's origins lie back in the mid-1990s, when the National Lottery's first flush of youth gave vent to many wild imaginings. Cornwall's geographic position may be isolated from the rest of Britain, but it also makes for interesting botanical possibilities; its geology may allow mining for china clay, but worked-out pits make unpleasant eyesores. Tim Smit had already exploited the county's botanical possibilities in creating the Lost Gardens of Heligan and, together with his initial partner in the enterprise, Cornish architect Jonathan Ball, conceived of a spectacular botanical collection that would explain the relationship of humans to plants across the world. It would require vast greenhouses, not just to recreate the climatic conditions of the tropics and the temperate zones, but also to allow plants to grow to their full size – something no existing glasshouse permitted. Using a redundant china-clay pit would avoid undue impact on landscape, as well as affording extra shelter to temperate or tropical plants, and

recycling an industrial site would add to the cocktail of funding available from European, local and national government bodies as well as the Millennium Commission. They duly identified the Bodelva pit, 5 kilometres east of St Austell, as a potential site, and commissioned Nicholas Grimshaw and Partners and engineers Anthony Hunt Associates to produce the eye-catching design necessary to secure lottery funding.

It was the 'Waterloo International Terminal' team, and the initial proposals recalled that magnificent, and then only recently completed, rail shed. Giant arched trusses of varying sizes extended from the bottom of the pit to the cliff face. But this design could not be finalised until excavations ceased, and excavations would not end until the pit could be bought – which in turn needed money which would not be forthcoming without a design. Grimshaw's job architect, Jolyon Brewis, remembers his colleague David Kirkland saying, 'We're not going to get there with fixed points top and bottom, so let's look at balls embedded in the earth'.

'With a geodesic dome', says Tony Hunt, 'you can alter the perimeter, especially if it's based on a hexagon.' The dome could adapt to variable and unpredictable ground conditions, an added advantage given that these comprised 'four grades of so-called rock'. Hunt explains that, 'geologically it's granite but that's all you can say', the weakest grade being 'in effect, mud'. In Hunt's opinion these difficult soil conditions made 'the civil engineering ... more complex than the dome'. Geodesic domes are variations of a generic solution, drawing on a large and existing body

Below left
Before cladding, the two-tier structure was clearly visible. The inner layer forms interlocking triangles and hexagons to the outer layer's hexagons, with occasional pentagons to absorb geometric anomalies. Spanning up to 11 metres the cladding panels are at the limit of possible size. Structural elements are kept to a minimum to achieve the highest possible transmission of light, but make a spectacular enclosure.

Below right, top
The ETFE cushions with three layers of foil were made by Foiltec in Bremen, Germany. They are inflated cushions, strong enough to walk on and easy to repair or replace. Testing proved that their performance would be satisfactory.

Below right, middle
Site progress at January 2000. After excavations ceased 800,000 cubic metres of earth were moved to regrade and stabilise the pit for roads, paths and car parks as well as for areas for growing plants, worked out with landscape architects Land Use Consultants. In keeping with the centre's ambitions to be a 'green' project as little material as possible was moved off or on to the site. Rainwater is retained for irrigation and humidity – only drinking water is brought to the centre.

Below right, bottom
Analysis diagram of the humid tropics biome under snow loading. The possibility of drifting snow in the 'valleys' between the domes necessitated additional cable-net reinforcement. The inflation of the cushions can be increased under sustained load.

Site plan
1 Humid tropics biome: plants from Amazonia, West Africa, Malaysia and Oceania
2 Warm temperate biome: plants from California, southern Africa and the Mediterranean
3 Landscaped grounds: the story of plants from temperate climates such as that of the UK
4 Visitor centre with gallery, restaurant and shops
5 Lake
6 Main car park
7 Amphitheatre for 2,300 spectators
8 Restaurant at the Centre of the World

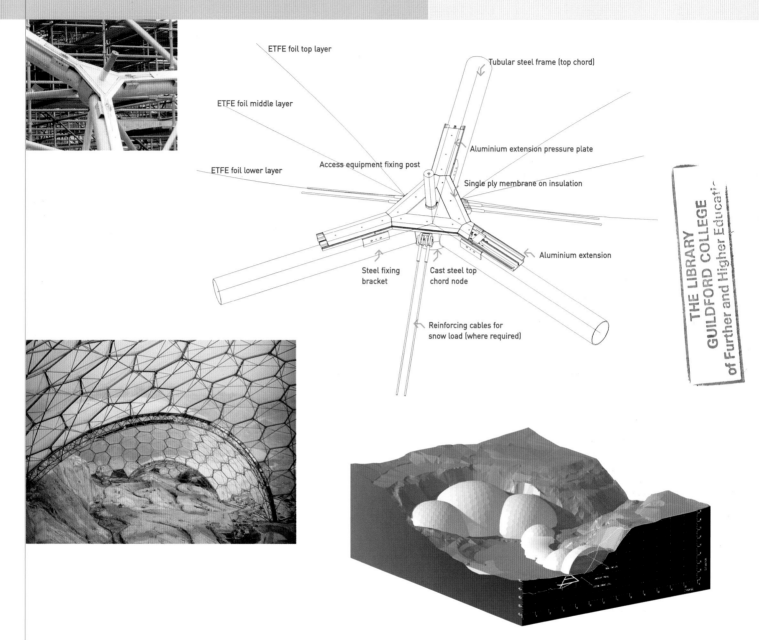

of experience and knowledge. The ground conditions meant that constructing foundations – including a concrete 'necklace' under the perimeter of the buildings – moving 800,000 cubic metres of soil and developing a system of water-holding beds to deal with rain- and ground-water without exceeding the permitted outflow called for unique, contingent solutions.

One effect of these ground conditions was to reinforce the programme's demand for a lightweight structure, leading to a process which Jolyon Brewis describes. The Eden Project, he says, 'sits in the tradition of great glasshouses'. He mentions the orangery at Chatsworth where Joseph Paxton cut his teeth before the Crystal Palace, a wonderfully elegant filigree at Lichtenstein Castle, and railway examples such as Barlow's shed at St Pancras. What they all have in common, he argues, is that they all aimed to make an enclosure which was as light and transparent as possible, given the materials, construction and structural knowledge of the day. All used glass, and most

used wrought and cast iron. Their equivalents now are aluminium and ETFE, which has less than 1 per cent of the weight of glass and can come in panels of up to 11 square metres compared to glass's maximum size of 2 by 4 metres. ETFE, used as inflated cushions, also has good transmission for visible and ultraviolet light. Glass would need to be double-glazed, increasing the complexity of installation and capacity of lifting equipment, as well as the final weight. With larger panels than have ever been built before, and the largest biome for the humid tropics environment spanning 110 metres and rising 56 metres, these are geodesic domes to match, if not Bucky Fuller's famous proposal to roof over Manhattan, at least those that have actually been constructed.

Such innovation demanded careful analysis and development. At the tender stage for the envelope,

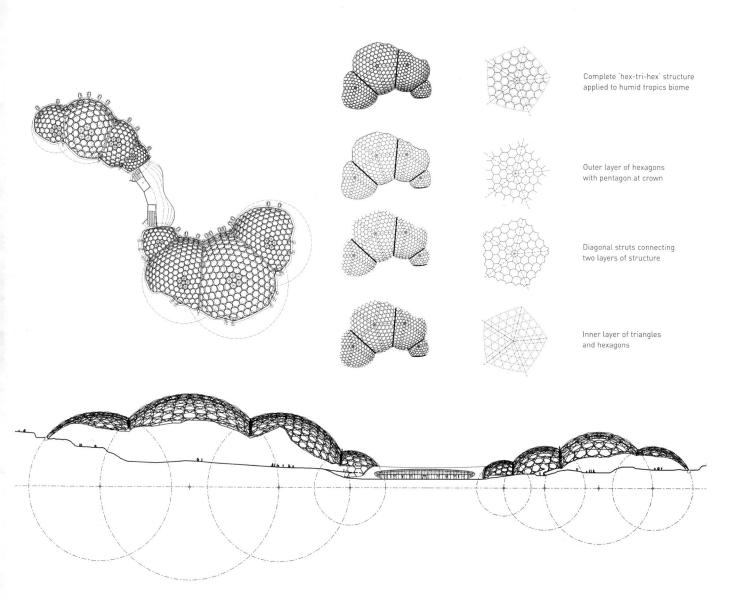

Complete 'hex-tri-hex' structure
applied to humid tropics biome

Outer layer of hexagons
with pentagon at crown

Diagonal struts connecting
two layers of structure

Inner layer of triangles
and hexagons

the design called for a single-layer structure with steel sections 500 millimetres in diameter to hold the aluminium and ETFE-cushion cladding system. The successful tenderer, the German company Mero, suggested a two-tier structure based on a system they have developed over many years, with outer members of less than 200 millimetres in diameter and inner tubes of 114 millimetres in diameter. The resultant structure, of hexagons and the odd pentagon on the outer skin and triangles and hexagons for the inner, makes a fine three-dimensional filigree without compromising the effect of lightness and transparency. A zone of diagonal struts connects the two layers of structure.

On the outside of the outer structure are the ETFE cushions with three layers of foil. Made by Foiltec of Bremen in Germany (and subcontracted to Mero), they weigh about 15 kilograms per square metre and are held on to the steel frame by aluminium extrusions. Although ETFE is now relatively familiar,

and some installations are 20 years old, the size of the cushions at Eden broke new ground in performance criteria and needed considerable development including physical tests and mock-ups. Their lightness makes maintenance and replacement relatively simple. Wind-tunnel tests showed that, because the structures are in a pit below ground level, wind loads are rather less than expected. However, snow loads, especially with the possibility of snow accumulating in the valleys between the domes, required an auxiliary cable-stay structure.

Tony Hunt recalls that the geodesic domes' smallest peculiarity 'would provoke a four-hour dissertation from Bucky'. In finding solutions to the oddities of the site at Eden – a subterranean pit with unstable ground conditions – Hunt, Grimshaw and their suppliers have gone beyond what even Buckminster Fuller envisaged. ⌂

Zombory-Moldovan Moore

Adam Zombory-Moldovan is an architect who looks for parallels in art rather than architecture for his own work, while remaining resolute in his architectural preoccupations – materials, space and context. As Helen Castle found out, when she visited his London office, it is an approach that has allowed the practice to pursue very specific solutions to individual projects and to produce an output of amazing diversity.

The singular and the idiosyncratic have often been regarded as characteristic of British art. The works of the greatest modern artists – Francis Bacon, Freud, Howard Hodgkin and Stanley Spencer – have been nourished on their own internal visions and personal references. Architecture, in contrast, tends to veer away from discussions of the personal, to the point of disowning the subjective and denying the contribution that individual tastes and preferences make. Adam Zombory-Moldovan, principal of London practice Zombory-Moldovan Moore, is a refreshing exception. Rejecting the current tendency to overconceptualise, and the obsession with the theoretical and the diagrammatic, he acknowledges the importance of the individual. He regards the sort of 'subjective likes' that are generally underplayed in 'serious' architectural discussions as 'critical' – proving essential to lively debate in his office during the design process.[1] What is clear from talking to him is that this insistence on one-to-one engagement in design demands a rare coherence of thought specific to each project. This does not allow him to fall back on the given or accepted, or an abstracted platform for thinking, which theory so often provides. Programme, situation and material context are explored in a fresh, inclusive way.

Since founding the office in 1990 with the architectural journalist Rowan Moore, Zombory-Moldovan has nurtured a profound, individual approach to architecture. The seeds of this were sewn at Cambridge, where he undertook both parts of his architectural education. There he was taught by Eric Parry, Dalibor Vesely and Peter Carl; Parry was largely responsible for fostering his interest in spaces as settings

and the importance of the interior, and Carl for an understanding of the significance of the cultural and urban context. Subsequently Zombory-Moldovan developed his own specific preoccupations with buildings' material presence and atmosphere. It seems that from an early stage he had resolved to follow his own instincts and develop his own work. For instance, on graduating he chose his first jobs for the sort of skills and opportunities they offered rather than for the type of architecture the office practised. In 1997, when he returned to Cambridge to run a diploma unit, he set up a new programme to stimulate ideas about material presence: he introduced students to sites in neglected parts of London, such as Shoreditch Park and a disused railway line, and asked them to seek potential in their existing physical presence or form. This was a new departure for Cambridge at the time and, through acts of making, his students worked from material intimacy to large-scale urban intervention.

A more fundamental watershed in his own practice, however, had already occurred five years earlier, when Rowan Moore left Zombory-Moldovan Moore to take up the editorship of Blueprint and concentrate on journalism full time. This afforded Zombory-Moldovan a fresh opportunity to focus on and develop his own architectural interests.

In his design practice Zombory-Moldovan is intrigued by the potential of the familiar – to be both explored and transformed. Each building is an act of invention where

Below
Department store project, New Delhi, 1995. A 25,000-square-foot shoe store designed for the bustling Karol Bagh shopping district of New Delhi. The interior is structured as a landscape public space with an arena on one level, a lake-like open rectangle on another and a catwalk and restaurant on the top floor.

brief, form and materials are manipulated and exploited to reveal richness and surprise in the familiar. His designs expose uncanny properties of material and space, undermining the expected, to create buildings with extraordinary presence and atmosphere.

On the surface, Zombory-Moldovan's interests do not appear wholly architectural. He prefers to make parallels with art over architecture. This is largely borne out by his particular interest in material substance and in atmosphere, and how these relate to form and programme. This is a territory of investigation pursued by artists such as Joseph Beuys and Rachel Whiteread. For Beuys, the transformability and indeterminate nature of fat as a material led him to manipulate and explore it, pressed into the corners of a room or piled over a radiator; this disturbs and redirects one's knowledge of the material, its meanings and properties. In art installation *House* Whiteread exploited the capacity of cast materials to record and define, and in so doing disrupted but intensified our preconceptions of the dwelling.

Nevertheless, Zombory-Moldovan cautions that a clear distinction between art and architecture should be retained. When the practice, for instance, hit the headlines with their Oil Room installation for the RIBA in 1998, they were asked by a CNN news reporter whether they were trying to make art. Zombory-Moldovan is adamant that architects should not try to be artists, as their main preoccupation should be with space. His own concerns are concentrated on how materials create or make space – materials being the main physical medium. Material decisions, therefore, are fundamental to the practice's thinking about space, form and atmosphere. Rather than falling back on a 'perceived palette' of materials – whether it be the fashionable or the expected architectural vocabulary of a specific office – at Zombory-Moldovan Moore each material is chosen and used as the substance of the building. The choice depends on the expected and familiar as well as the potential for the unpredictable. This enables the

Below
The Oil Room, RIBA, London, 1998. This gallery-sized installation was designed to question familiar notions of comfort by exploring luxury and danger. At its centre was an inner room surrounded by walls of cascading hydraulic oil. Mesmerising and beautiful to watch, the oil was thick and repulsive to touch. Yet this inner space was luxurious with a soft, upholstered leather floor and a low, artificial fur-lined ceiling, gentle, warm light coming through the oil walls.

material to be used to surprise or enrich, allowing it to perform in a less expected way to affect the nature of space.

What is clear is that in their design practice Zombory-Moldovan Moore focus on introducing invention through intellectual rigour, thinking through each aspect of a design as part of a diverse but coherent whole. This does not only come through in their choice of materials but also in their response to the individual brief of each commission. By eschewing the 'wow factor', which is so prevalent in so much contemporary architecture, they concentrate on tuning the quality of atmosphere for a particular building's activity. This is most apparent in the work they have done for art galleries. Rather than adopting the now common vocabulary of large expanses of white walls contrasted with bare concrete, wood or stone, they reinvent each gallery space for its particular context and collection; as Zombory-Moldovan states, richness need not be measured against blandness or neutrality. For Sam Fogg Rare Books and Manuscripts, the office created a long gallery space with further smaller libraries and viewing spaces opening off it. The gallery space was designed to carefully orchestrate the relationship between the main space and its subsidiary spaces in terms of darkness and light, and natural light and artificial light. Within the main gallery, there was set up a dramatic contrast between a pale, daylit viewing area and a long, dark, artificially lit space at the other end. Shifts in emphasis of materials, textures and light are made to transform the atmosphere without fragmenting the whole. The dark space was lined with a coarse purple silk

stretched over wall panels, which played on the richness and ornateness of the items on display.

The 'interconnectedness of spaces', where the material formation of each space is carefully tuned to those connected and adjacent to it, is a recurring theme in Zombory-Moldovan's work. This is particularly marked at the Philpott House at Knocknacolon, County Cork, where two adjoining blocks were created to meet the client's concurrent needs for open and public spaces at meal times, for feeding farm workers, with a sequence of more private sitting and sleeping spaces. The rural setting of the house provided a further opportunity for connectedness allowing the practice to set up a relationship between the interior and the exterior, and the artificial and the natural landscape.

After only 10 years in practice, it is undisputable that Zombory-Moldovan's unstinting rigour, with its emphasis on atmosphere and materials, is paying off. His work is bringing to fruition his goal of creating a rich and potent architecture which has the substance to change the social and physical circumstances of its users. His references are broad and inclusive, but the results are unexpected, stimulating and focused, making gorgeous spaces for contemporary life. ∆

Note
1. Quoted from a talk by Adam Zombory-Moldovan given at Kingston University, December 2000.

Below

Philpott House, Knocknacolon, County Cork, 1997–99. This house in southwest Ireland is located on the slope of a valley adjacent to an early Christian ring fort. Conceived as a series of linked structures, it creates protected outside spaces while being embedded in the landscape. The client required both public spaces for the farm workers and more private living spaces for herself and her parents. The house accommodates these two functions in two distinct blocks. The distinction is emphasised by the contrasting colours and textures of the exterior: whereas one block is dry-stone walled, connecting it to the ground, with a large glazed corner to the southeast, the other block is a smooth blue-painted render – a colour that connects it to the sky. Overall, the look of the house is one in which familarity is disrupted by the unexpected. The familiar rural, pitched-roofed barn type has here been fragmented and dismembered into separate parts that reconnect as you move around the buildings.

Young People's Cultural Centre, Marble Arch, London, 1999-. This project for an underground cultural centre brings together three organisations – an art gallery, a museum and a youth group – and will include an auditorium, art galleries, museum, conference spaces, restaurant, café and shop. Zombory-Moldovan Moore's scheme for the project centres on the idea of creating interconnectedness between the specific activities of the place such as visiting the galleries, with less defined activities such as meeting, eating and drinking. By using transparency and layering of structure and activity, the conventional boundaries between controlled arts spaces and foyers is to be blurred. Light and transparency is at the core of the scheme. A glass box containing a café-performance space is suspended over the museum and gallery, shedding light across a foyer and down into the exhibition spaces. The foyer is a long open space with a café and seating. A light-shedding information wall, with shifting texts and images, runs the length of the space in a shallow curve. The café light box and information wall act as points of orientation and combine to provide an intensity of light that is a substitute for the windows and views generally found in overground spaces.

Resumé

1990	Practice founded by Adam Zombory-Moldovan and Rowan Moore
	New house, Sussex
	Theatre space, Edinburgh
	Feasibility projects: Chinese Cultural Centre, hotel & offices, Budapest
1991	Aberdeen studios and workshops, Highbury, London
1992	Musicians' and painters' studios, London
1993	Holdsworth House, London workshop building, Dorset
1994	Carnevale Restaurant and Deli, Barbican, London
1995	Steane House, Office fit-out Bleeding Heart Yard, Hatton Garden, London
1993–97	Restaurants and public areas for Sotheby's, London
1994–97	Himalayan, Southeast Asian, Islamic and medals galleries for Spink & Son Ltd
1994	Sam Fogg galleries for medieval manuscripts and artefacts, London
1995	Department stores and shoe retail projects in New Delhi, India
1996	Private galleries for art collector, Holland Park
1997–99	Philpott House, Knocknacolon, County Cork
	Adam Zombory-Moldovan runs diploma unit at Cambridge
1997	Capsule hotel projects, London
1998	Oil Room installation at the RIBA
	Selected by the Architecture Foundation for the book and exhibition, 'Britain's Best Young Architectural Practices'.
1999	Young People's Cultural Centre, Marble Arch, London
2000	Public square, Saltaire, West Yorkshire
	New galleries for Sam Fogg, Cork Street, London
2001	Deli projects, Borough Market, London
	Simon Dickinson old master and modern galleries, Jermyn Street, London
	Watts Gallery, Compton, Surrey

Book Reviews

Architectural Supermodels
by Tom Porter & John Neale,
Architectural Press (Oxford), 2000,
186 pages, £29.99

4+1 Peter Salter Building Projects
with essays by Peter Beardsell,
Robert Harbison and Andrew Higgott,
Black Dog Publishing (London), 1999,
96 pages, £19.95

I have tried, so far unsuccessfully, to persuade my students at RWTH, Aachen, to not only produce those beautiful white models, which so convince their peers and their other professors, but also to use development models that convey their early conceptual ideas.

The success of this book, developed as part of a major study by the diploma course at Oxford Brookes University, is that it describes so well the use of models in all their forms. They range from those that allow clients to visualise the actual spaces, like that of the banking hall for the Hong Kong Bank, to more modest examples, which stimulate conversation about design possibilities, such as the working models by Roderick Coyne for Will Alsop.

Beautifully laid out by John Neale, it describes the emergence of professional supermodel-makers, including Andrew Ingram, Chris Barber, Ademir Voller and Don Shuttleworth, and points to their importance in supporting architectural exploration of form and detail.

I would have welcomed more description of the use of full-scale prototypes as developed by Nicholas Grimshaw for Waterloo International and the Eden Project, and the use of trial mouldings of full-size parts of an assembly. This kind of experimental method was used to great effect by Renzo Piano in the detailing of the Bercy Charenton Shopping Centre in Paris; and I always remember Tony Hunt making a model of the proposed roof for the Faber Dumas Headquarters by Chris Wilkinson at lunchtime, using his pipe cleaners to assist the afternoon discussion.

Supermodels offers a fascinating insight into the working methods of the architectural practices of Frank Gehry and Will Alsop and shows how the realisation of projects such as Bilbao and Alsop's c/plex project, which are born as sketches or paintings, evolve through successive design models and finally lead to, in Gehry's case, physical modelling being scanned into the computer and digitised into an electronic version of itself.

The authors often refer to the use of illusion. Remember that Rudolf Luscher once won the International Housing Competition on the basis of photographs of models, published in the Architectural Review (March 1989), which were so convincing they persuaded the competition jury in the US that they were judging a built scheme.

In the end this is a book about virtual reality, stunningly presented with a hint of Alice in Wonderland. It is a welcome contribution to the debate on alternative ways of presenting architectural ideas. *Alan J Brooke*

This book was destined to be beautiful. Peter Salter's intricate drawings, sketch models and paintings are visually stunning and evocative. These illustrations interweave three essays and short project-related texts to describe five projects by the architect and teacher: four in Japan and one for Glasgow City of Architecture.

As Andrew Higgott says, 'The translation from drawn project to building in the work of Peter Salter was . . . long awaited.' This publication is ultimately about the process of this translation, what Peter Salter feels he has learnt from it and how the essayists - all 'critics, cajolers and chroniclers' of his work - perceive what he has achieved. Often quite personal insights, they read easily as distinct pieces.

Visually, one can read quite clearly from 'as built' photographs that Peter Salter's distinctive buildings encapsulate the essence of the drawings in which they were imagined. The less clear, but particularly intriguing, area of the process is a set of rules that Salter himself describes as the tools he uses to underpin the complex forms and materiality of his buildings. It seems paradoxical that 'rules' are used here to create such a morphic, almost animate architecture. Although the subject is touched upon, a more thorough exploration of the background and usage of these defining parameters, how Salter works with and against them, would be very welcome. What one does sense is that the architect is not shackled by his process. In fact, he describes at length how his process and preconceptions have been challenged and reshaped through his recent experience in building, particularly in the context of Japan and its culture.

The pieces included in this absorbing publication have obviously been carefully assembled. Interestingly, and perhaps consciously, there are frustratingly few coherent photographs of built work alongside the projections of their forms. Such descriptions, a definite second-best to the experience of the real architecture, could still be a useful tool in beginning to understand the important relationship between site and Salter's sited. In a positive way, the book leaves you curious to know more. *Sally Godwin*

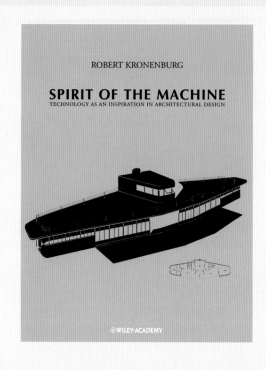

SPIRIT OF THE MACHINE: TECHNOLOGY AS
AN INSPIRATION IN ARCHITECTURAL DESIGN
Robert Kronenburg

PB 0 471 97860 4; £19.99; 279 x 217 mm; 136 pages; July 2001

Spirit of the Machine explores the importance of technological advance in architectural design and the spirit and philosophies that have inspired its aesthetic and symbolic development. It examines the expression of technology in the built and manufactured environment, focusing on current and future developments but also examining the significant legacy of traditional and historic architecture. The book makes use of a holistic approach to engage a topic that concerns wide-ranging issues of global concern which, nevertheless, impact on every individual.

Architecture is an intrinsic component of the way people identify their presence in the world. However, its meaning in this context is frequently overlooked in its role as an expedient tool. It is generally acknowledged that most contemporary architecture utilises technology in a haphazard manner. Many of us perceive that there is a confusion of architectural 'styles' that are used regardless of function or geographic location. The relationship between occupant, environment and resources which forms the fundamental balance that leads to the design of successful buildings is under threat – the result is international 'no-place' architecture. Many people, not without reason, feel that advances in technology are a root cause of the proliferation of this anonymous environment. Some have therefore suggested that the solution is to return to simple traditional buildings and craftsman-based design methods. This, however, ignores the irreversible impact that technological innovation has on society, and cannot be the basis for any widespread, long-term solution.

Recent technological innovations in the construction process have primarily been incorporated as grafted-on elements in existing building methods. In many cases the ultimate goals of building provision remain short term with success often evaluated in terms of economic return. However, technological advance is an integral factor in the development of building design which, if utilised in an appropriate manner, has the potential to lead to high-quality architecture that is also economic and sensitive. It is a paradox that although technological change is very visible and often dramatic, the basic requirements of the human beings who generate that change are not. The primary principles of security, comfort and beauty remain the core elements of architectural design. Perhaps the nature of these timeless elements does not need to be revolutionised – it is only in their recognition and creation as part of an appropriate building strategy for contemporary resources and situations that change is necessary.

Spirit of the Machine explores the relationship between the two areas of human-made activity that impact on contemporary life most profoundly: the application of science and the design of our environment. Though the book examines the possibilities for new design approaches which exploit innovative and alternative technologies that may widen designers' horizons and increase their ability to create appropriate settings for contemporary life, it is not a study of technology itself. Rather, it is an exploration of its effect on a fundamental aspect of human existence: how we inhabit the world. The book's objective is to evaluate the way in which technological advances in the field of building can be synthesised into an architecture that is useful, meaningful and beautiful – characteristics that will enable it to establish the sense of place necessary to maintain the continuity of human identity. △D

Edwin Heathcote, the author of *Cinema Builders*
(Wiley-Academy), 2001, describes one of the
most exciting and revolutionary moving picture house
designs of the 20th century.

Cinema?
Pictures, theatre of motion!
Motion is life,
Real life is genuine, simple and true,
Therefore no affectation, no sentimentality.
Not in the pictures, not on the screen, not in the building …
No sober reality, no claustrophobia of life-weary brain acrobats – Fantasy!
Fantasy – but no lunatic asylum – dominated by space, colour and light.
All planes, curves and light waves flash from the ceiling to the screen through
the medium of music into the flickering image – into the Universe.

These extracts are from a poem by Erich Mendelsohn, a paean
to the inauguration of his Universum cinema on Berlin's
Kurfürstendamm in 1929. Metropolis, Fritz Lang's nightmare
vision of the future, was released in the year in which
Mendelsohn started working on the Universum (1926). It was
the first film to use the Schufftan Process (it was all done with
mirrors) which allowed live action and model sets to be
juxtaposed effectively for the first time, enabling the creation
of truly visionary worlds on film. A year after that, The Jazz
Singer appeared, the first film to use sound. The most
extravagant era of Expressionism in both film and architecture
had ended and Mendelsohn, whose Potsdam Einstein Tower of
1920 was perhaps the zenith of Expressionism in architecture,
had turned to a sleek, streamlined architecture which was the
embodiment of his dramatically elemental thumbnail sketches.

The Universum Cinema is, in effect, a built realisation of
one of Mendelsohn's characteristic sketches. Yet it is no mere
Expressionistic gesture. The building was almost without
precedent in that its external form closely followed the internal
functions. Cinema architecture had essentially derived from
theatre architecture and the differences in function were often
not acknowledged in tectonic form. In stripping away the fussy
decoration ('No rococo-castle … No stucco pastries') of the
traditional theatrical building type, Mendelsohn acknowledged
the power of the screen. People may have gone to the theatre
to watch the audience, and the high-society figures ensconced
in the boxes, as much as the actors on the stage; the cinema,
however, was a more democratic forum where the image on
the screen ruled supreme. The horseshoe-shaped auditorium
was expressed in a sleek, wrap-around curve and the
continuous ribbon window which followed this around
illuminated the circulation spaces which encircled the
auditorium and brought the irresistible life of the building
to the street. A slim fin broke through this curve affording
purpose-built space for advertising and lighting (avoiding the
problems of applied signage ruining the original architectural
intention).

The whole interior of the Universum seemed to be rushing
at speed towards the screen; sleek, illuminated lines gave a

directionality to the interior and a sense of artifice and
excitement while never detracting from the focus of the
space: the screen. Mendelsohn's version of expressive
streamlining greatly influenced buildings during the
1930s and specifically struck a deep chord with
British cinema architects, although Britain, as a whole,
remained immune to the sculptural excesses of
Expressionism. Mendelsohn's curving, sketch-like
forms were a clear influence on WE Trent's streamlined
Gaumont Palace, Wolverhampton (1932), Alistair
Gladstone Macdonald's curvaceous and dynamic
newsreel theatre built within Victoria Station (1934),
the elegant fluting of Wamsley Lewis's New Victoria
just around the corner and a host of others. Indeed
Mendelsohn's most characteristic architectonic device,
the solid vertical fin cutting through the streamlined
forms of the building (which was also used to expel
exhaust air), would prove hugely influential and
inspired Harry Weedon's Odeons of the 1930s, buildings
which remain perhaps the greatest and most influential
series of cinema buildings.

Bearing in mind that the Universum was among the
first buildings to recognise the need for a fundamentally
different mode of design for cinemas than that used for
theatres, it is a supreme irony that perhaps the greatest
modern cinema building is now used as a theatre.
It was damaged during the Second World War and
subsequently badly neglected. In 1978 it was extensively
reconstructed for use as a highly adaptable theatre and
it has become, perhaps surprisingly, a great success.
Its expressive but pared down curves remain the acme
of Modernism where building is integrated into the
cityscape and cinema (or theatre) is made truly urban,
where night and day, interior and exterior, are blended
into a single experience. To quote Mendelsohn's poem:

Under the swinging circle of the foyer, the street
disappears, under the conical beams of the ceiling
lights, the haze of evening disappears.

AD

Subscribe Now for 2001

As an influential and prestigious architectural publication, *Architectural Design* has an almost unrivalled reputation worldwide. Published bi-monthly, it successfully combines the currency and topicality of a newsstand journal with the editorial rigour and design qualities of a book. Consistently at the forefront of cultural thought and design since the 60s, it has time and again proved provocative and inspirational – inspiring theoretical, creative and technological advances. Prominent in the 80s for the part it played in Post-Modernism and then Deconstruction, Δ has recently taken a pioneering role in the technological revolution of the 90s. With ground-breaking titles dealing with cyberspace and hypersurface architecture, it has pursued the conceptual and critical implications of high-end computer software and virtual realities. Δ

Δ Architectural Design

SUBSCRIPTION RATES 2001
Institutional Rate: UK £150
Personal Rate: UK £97
Discount Student* Rate: UK £70
OUTSIDE UK
Institutional Rate: US $225
Personal Rate: US $145
Student* Rate: US $105

*Proof of studentship will be required when placing an order. Prices reflect rates for a 2001 subscription and are subject to change without notice.

TO SUBSCRIBE
Phone your credit card order:
UK/Europe: +44 (0)1243 843 828
USA: +1 212 850 6645
Fax your credit card order to:
UK/Europe: +44 (0)1243 770 432
USA: +1 212 850 6021

Email your credit card order to:
cs-journals@wiley.co.uk
Post your credit card or cheque order to:

UK/Europe: John Wiley & Sons Ltd.
Journals Administration Department
1 Oldlands Way
Bognor Regis
West Sussex PO22 9SA
UK

USA: John Wiley & Sons Ltd.
Journals Administration Department
605 Third Avenue
New York, NY 10158
USA

Please include your postal delivery address with your order.

All Δ volumes are available individually.
To place an order please write to:
John Wiley & Sons Ltd
Customer Services
1 Oldlands Way
Bognor Regis
West Sussex PO22 9SA

Please quote the ISBN number of the issue(s) you are ordering.

Δ is available to purchase on both a subscription basis and as individual volumes

---

○ I wish to subscribe to Δ Architectural Design at the **Institutional rate of £150.**

○ I wish to subscribe to Δ Architectural Design at the **Personal rate of £97.**

○ I wish to subscribe to Δ Architectural Design at the **Student rate of £70.**

STARTING FROM ISSUE 1/2001.

○ Payment enclosed by Cheque/Money order/Drafts.

Value/Currency £/US$ [＿＿＿＿＿]

○ Please charge £/US$ [＿＿＿＿＿] to my credit card.

Account number:

[▢▢▢▢▢▢▢▢▢▢▢▢▢▢▢▢▢▢]

Expiry date:

[▢▢▢▢▢▢]

Card: Visa/Amex/Mastercard/Eurocard *(delete as applicable)*

Cardholder's signature [＿＿＿＿＿＿＿]

Cardholder's name [＿＿＿＿＿＿＿]

Address [＿＿＿＿＿＿＿]

[＿＿＿＿＿＿＿]

[＿＿＿＿＿] Post/Zip Code [＿＿＿＿]

Recepient's name [＿＿＿＿＿＿＿]

Address [＿＿＿＿＿＿＿]

[＿＿＿＿＿＿＿]

[＿＿＿＿＿] Post/Zip Code [＿＿＿＿]

I would like to buy the following Back Issues at £19.99 each:

○ Δ 151 *New Babylonians*, Iain Borden + Sandy McCreery

○ Δ 150 *Architecture + Animation*, Bob Fear

○ Δ 149 *Young Blood*, Neil Spiller

○ Δ 148 *Fashion and Architecture*, Martin Pawley

○ Δ 147 *The Tragic in Architecture*, Richard Patterson

○ Δ 146 *The Transformable House*, Jonathan Bell and Sally Godwin

○ Δ 145 *Contemporary Processes in Architecture*, Ali Rahim

○ Δ 144 *Space Architecture*, Dr Rachel Armstrong

○ Δ 143 *Architecture and Film II*, Bob Fear

○ Δ 142 *Millennium Architecture*, Maggie Toy and Charles Jencks

○ Δ 141 *Hypersurface Architecture II*, Stephen Perrella

○ Δ 140 *Architecture of the Borderlands*, Teddy Cruz

○ Δ 139 *Minimal Architecture II*, Maggie Toy

○ Δ 138 *Sci-Fi Architecture*, Maggie Toy

○ Δ 137 *Des-Res Architecture*, Maggie Toy

○ Δ 136 *Cyberspace Architecture II*, Neil Spiller

○ Δ 135 *Ephemeral/Portable Architecture*, Robert Kronenburg

○ Δ 134 *The Everyday and Architecture*, Sarah Wigglesworth

○ Δ 133 *Hypersurface Architecture*, Stephen Perrella

○ Δ 132 *Tracing Architecture*, Nikos Georgiadis

○ Δ 131 *Consuming Architecture*, Sarah Chaplin and Eric Holding